Re-Visioning The Way We Work

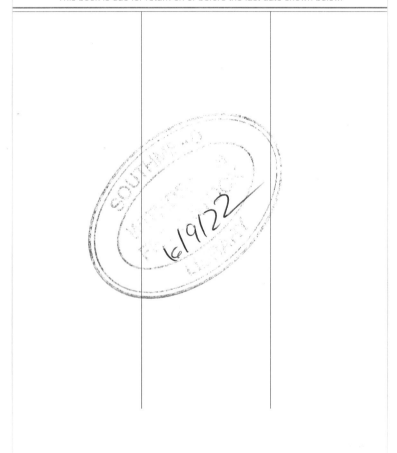

Re-Visioning The Way We Work

✦

A Heroic Journey

Ginger Grant PhD.

iUniverse, Inc.
New York Lincoln Shanghai

Re-Visioning The Way We Work
A Heroic Journey

iUniverse books may be ordered through booksellers or by contacting:

iUniverse
2021 Pine Lake Road, Suite 100
Lincoln, NE 68512
www.iuniverse.com
1-800-Authors (1-800-288-4677)

ISBN-13: 978-0-595-36595-1 (pbk)
ISBN-13: 978-0-595-81024-6 (ebk)
ISBN-10: 0-595-36595-7 (pbk)
ISBN-10: 0-595-81024-1 (ebk)

Printed in the United States of America

No book is ever birthed alone and this one is no exception. I am blessed with an amazing group of friends that continually nourish both my body and soul.

This book is lovingly dedicated in their honour.

*Janet Anderson, grandmother extraordinaire
the first to teach me that no one you love ever dies…
they simply become portable.*

Judith Bertoia

Tina Giallonardo
Kenton Hyatt
George McEwen
David Miller
Paula Palmer
Janice Pass
Shirley Poole
Michael Ray
Joe Rea
Dennis Patrick Slattery
Annie, Jerry and Luna Schaffer

*To the students and faculty at Pacifica Graduate Institute
and other followers of archetypal psychology,
I also dedicate this book.
My hope is that those who follow gain further insight for the journey
and help me correct any wrong turns on the map.
Any errors or omissions are mine alone.*

Contents

Preface

Cheryl De Ciantis
Santa Cruz, July 2005.

Every life—and every organization—is mythic territory. If you have ever worked for a beastly or a memorably empowering boss, survived re-organization or suffered redundancy, worked on a dead-end and disheartened and disheartening team or a collaborative, mutually supportive and beyond-all-expectations successful one, you have lived a mythic pattern. Those and a thousand other workaday experiences are archetypal verities that play themselves out in the human psyche in grand spirals of repetition and elaboration. "If it's happened once," we say, "it's happened a thousand times."

Many people learned about myth as an idea and as a way of life from Joseph Campbell. *The Power of Myth* television series, based on conversations between Campbell and journalist Bill Moyers, first aired on PBS in the US in 1988, a year after Campbell's death. It sent powerful waves of recognition through North American culture and influenced a generation.

Campbell's best-known book, *The Hero With a Thousand Faces*, sets forward the idea that each of us lives through a hero's—or heroine's—journey that is both new and very, very old. No wonder this idea captured the imaginations of millions: we see it in every day life. As Campbell pointed out, "The latest incarnation of Oedipus, the continued romance of Beauty and the Beast, stand this afternoon on the corner of Forty-second Street and Fifth Avenue, waiting for the traffic light to change."

Fascinating, recognizable, profound. But, applicable—particularly in regard to the so often painful and seemingly inescapable repetitions of the challenges of organizational life—even after the expensive attentions of armies of theorists and consultants? What does one *do* with this kind of insight?

Enter Ginger Grant, mythologist extraordinaire. What makes this book so extraordinary is that Grant's mythic scholarship is devoted to application in real lives—both the life of the corporate "person" and the lives of those who individually and collectively work and achieve within the corporate body. Grant delves into myth, and into depth psychology—the branch of psychology whose field of attention is the soul—to find out what *works*.

What works is story. Not just any story, but the story that is authentically felt and lived. And, while Grant recognizes the profound power of the Hero/ine's Journey myth for corporate life, this book is no facile telling of tales. Grant does not pull any punches by dumbing down the psychological subtleties or underestimating the dedication, determination and passion required to reach breakthrough.

Most of us recognize the dilemmas created when organizations venture into the territory of the archetype without a genuine connection with the Call. The result is an unpalatable and discouraging soup that was yesterday's *du jour*, whose ill odor can spoil the appetite for change for years to come. ("Oh, great. We're going to be "storied" again. Whatever.")

True engagement with the archetypal journey is transformative. Read this book to find out how to transform yourself and your organization.

Introduction

This book is born from frustration. My world is both the world of organizations and my ongoing fascination with the transformative power of archetypal psychology. I was searching for a way to bring the best of both together in order to offer a how-and-why-to book in using an archetypal or values-based approach to organizational development. This book is the result. It contains both the theory used to reach this point (so that other researchers may follow) and what archetypal psychology might offer for the future in organizational development (for those only interested in its direct practical application).

The source of creativity is in the human imagination. The birth of a corporation is a creative process that also has its origin in the same imagination. Every corporate story begins with an idea that becomes an expanded and shared vision. Before that vision is well shared, much less completely implemented, the organization must pass through a developmental process that is similar to all human development. In this sense, the growth of a corporation can be seen as a mythic journey. In these pages, I will explore how the Hero's Journey, described by mythologist Joseph Campbell, can be used as a tool for transformation in a corporate environment. Further, how a corporate culture might be better understood and enhanced through the use of this model.

Although players and circumstances vary with time and place, there remains something unalterable and true at the core of myths. Myths are not just told; they are *felt*, as they resonate throughout the body as well as the mind. Throughout the ages, the power of story has nourished the human soul; from this same level of passion a corporation may be created and should be maintained. Not all organizations are created to fulfill a noble passion; some seem to exist purely because of greed. As evidenced by recent events in corporate America, such organizations' ethical foundations are crumbling; corporations like Enron and WorldCom have lost touch with their own core stories. Assuming that such companies were founded upon stories of integrity, one might ask what went wrong. As Jungian Analyst James Hillman suggests "ideas we have, and do not know we have, have us."[1] In other words, if you don't know the myth you are living, then the myth lives you. Is it possible that if organizations lose awareness of foundational stories which contain fundamental operating principles, such organizations will flounder when they encounter difficulty? Perhaps the loss of such a powerful mythic foundation creates the difficulty in the first place.

Using a broad definition of creativity, to provide a corporate structure that is innovative and open to expansion is no less an artistic act than the creation of a symphony or a body of literature. Acts of creation have the power to touch people in ways that transcend verbal expression. In an organizational context, they have the potential to alter the environment whether locally, nationally, or even globally. As such, an act of creation has the potential to buffer change and, potentially, promote it.

After some years of success, many companies find themselves in the midst of many types of dynamic change (technological; economic, including marketplaces; workforce demographics; global and local politics) which prompt the need for change that goes beyond simple adaptation to an actual re-creation. Using the perspective of depth or archetypal psychology, a mythic map can be used by which an individual or a corporation can reconnect with the original, creative source. Such a move would result in a mythopoesis, a conscious re-visioning or re-making of myth. In an uncertain economic climate, with ever-increasing demographic shifts causing a shortage of people, an examination of corporate culture will provide current organizations with valuable strategic insight necessary not only to survive, but in fact to prosper.

Traditionally, an analysis of "corporate culture" is not part of a financial and legal due diligence process, but it is arguably fundamental to the success of an organization. The value of including cultural assessment in that process is both to insure compatibility with future partners and to make corporate leaders aware of the operational values in the organization. Values are not always well developed, much less well articulated; nonetheless, they do drive behavior. If a corporation is to be held to moral accountability, as seems evident in current events, the inherent moral structure must be part of some sort of investigation. This type of cultural analysis will have as much impact on an organization's future viability as do financial or structural considerations.

Why The Heroic Journey?

There is a significant discrepancy between current organizational development theory and the current practices of management in our organizations. In 1994, organizational theorist Ronald Heifetz addressed the problem of educating leaders along these lines. He stated that "the problem lies largely in their attitudes, values, habits, or current relationships; the problem-solving has to take place in their hearts and minds."[2] If the "hearts and minds" of these leaders are indeed the issue, then an operational framework involving both emotion and logic is in order. In *The Hero with a Thousand Faces,* Joseph Campbell describes such a model. Jungian Analyst James Hillman and others believe that the Heroic Journey needs re-visioning to be effective in today's changing world:

> Heroism is asked to face its own myth, thereby releasing the imagination to find other ways to think about power which has been defined for so long by heroic notions. Heroism, today, rather than focusing on turning problems around, has to turn itself around, inventing new ideas about the old heroics, re-visioning what *today* are the enemies of accomplishment. It is of little use to open bold new paths if you are still inside the same labyrinth. The model itself must break open.[3]

This book is my attempt to both break open and *re-vision* the Heroic Journey Model for organizational use. Albert Einstein was fond of saying that the thinking that got you in cannot be the thinking that gets you out. The visual map of the Heroic Journey can lead both organizations and the people who inhabit them, out of the current labyrinth. It is a unique and proven tool for transformation.

Need for Development of an Archetypal Model

Archetypal psychology is interdisciplinary, multivalent, and lends itself well to the exploration of different levels and contexts of relationship—personal and professional, as well as individual, group, and organizational. It can provide a nonthreatening framework for investigation, whether into the realm of corporate organization or the depths of the human psyche. Archetypal psychology can provide an inclusive environment of exploration based on a *both/and* approach to corporate challenges rather than the often divisive and shaming *either/or* approach so often characteristic of corporate milieus. As an examination of any archetype includes *both* extremes, a multiple lens is created. As Hillman explains,

> Using myths as grids lets you analyze phenomena by holding them up against the light of archetypal figures whose attributes and behaviors are even more complicated than what you are examining. Instead of reducing meaning to a definition, myths amplify and complicate. They are the path of richness.[4]

Instinctive factors, as outlined in Jung's metamythology, play a key role in bringing this "richness" to fruition. The Heroic Journey Model permits the holding of a corporate culture "against the light of archetypal figures." Campbell, for example, suggests "the hero is a man of self-achieved submission. But submission to what? That precisely is the riddle that today we have to ask ourselves and that it is everywhere the primary virtue and historic deed of the hero to be solved."[5] From an archetypal perspective, an examination of this primary heroic virtue provides insight into the study of a corporate culture. The utilization of the Heroic Journey as a path to a healthy personal psyche can then act as a mirror in the utilization of the Heroic Journey toward a healthy corporate psyche.

The consequences that result when a corporation's identity is not well developed, or founded on questionable values can be problematic. In such cases, it is difficult to maintain a value system that informs the corporation and maintains the relationship between upper management and employees in a positive and generative sense.

The current corporate practice of supposedly *empowering* employees through mission statements without ensuring that the mission statement remains connected to core values and objectives demands questioning. In a for-profit, especially stock-price-driven corporate culture, decades of hard-line, profit-margin mentality have eroded the possibility of a meaningful connection between corporate leaders and employees, as well as shared participation in a corporation's fundamental vision. Such disconnect in communication, driven by over-emphasis on profitability, ensures that the intellectual capital of individual employees does not reach full potential. Emphasis on short-term profitability denies the time needed to discover latent potential in individuals; nor does such lack of time permit alignment between management values and employee values in order to form a collective core.

Our mode of production has shifted to organizational knowledge creation. In this new economic environment, a traditional mode of production thinking is potentially counter-productive. A new paradigm is needed, one that recognizes that the future belongs to people who use their hearts as well as their heads. Awareness of this shift is the key to realizing a new paradigm. A corporate culture is a living mythology, which makes appropriate a depth psychological approach to ensure its well-being and survival, because the complexity of corporate culture cannot be understood from a superficial evaluation.

How Did We Get Here?
A Brief Review.

Jung states that "from the psychological standpoint five main groups of instinctive factors can be distinguished: hunger, sexuality, activity, reflection and creativity."[6] From these psychic instincts a metamythology emerges, a personal emotional construct that is the basis of beliefs and values, which in turn provides the interpretation in how we actually experience our myths. A more detailed elaboration of Jung's metamythology is contained in chapter 2. Each of the five aspects of the metamythology and its use, will be amplified in relation to the Heroic Journey Model in chapters 5-10. The origin of archetypal psychology have been attributed to the work of James Hillman and David Miller who expand this metamythology originally formulated by Jung.

In *The Myth of Analysis* Hillman argues: "history is only a doorway into further reflection."[7] According to Hillman, the emphasis is on delving deeper into both self and story, to find the original "archai," the first imprinting of an idea or image. This form of psychological approach attempts to identify the primary source of individual thinking and, as such, can provide clarity in the examination of corporate culture. It also provides the foundation for future branding.

In *Kinds of Power*, Hillman provides the psychological link between an archetypal approach and the world of business:

> Deepening forces an organization, like a marriage, to go into itself to get to the bottom of its troubles. Going to the bottom does not stop at the bottom line, but goes into those supporting myths and philosophies on which an organization—again, like a marriage—rests. What will be sacrificed to achieve its aims and to whose cost?[8]

Many business schools still teach that the purpose of an organization is profitability and thus concentrate on financial measurement and return on investment. The current trend is moving towards emphasizing the individual potential within the organization. In this more strategic model based on human capital retention, individuation of the knowledge worker is the prime concern, and the profitability of the corporation has a secondary focus. Such an emphasis does not preclude profitability, but permits both individual and organization a measure of success.

The Gallup organization has conducted extensive research on the importance of intellectual or human capital to the success of an organization. The initial research, based on surveys of over one million employees in the last twenty-five years, indicated that the length of time and level of productivity of an employee were directly related to the relationship between employee and manager. These results provided the impetus for a second set of research questions exploring how these successful managers retained valuable knowledge workers. Over eighty thousand managers were interviewed. The combination of these research studies conducted by Gallup provided the data for Marcus Buckingham and Curtis Coffman's *First, Break All the Rules* published in 1999.

Buckingham and Coffman suggest selecting an employee for overall talent rather than filling a specific job description. They outline how to set initial expectations, motivate workers, and implement employee development initiatives. Such an approach mirrors the process of individuation originally formulated by Jung. In this case, the manager consciously utilizes the process of individuation to maximize the ability of the employee. Although the language used is slightly different, the process is similar, but with an emphasis on the relationship between talent and performance. The authors emphasize discovering the unique aspects of each individual:

> Conventional wisdom is comforting, seductively easy. The revolutionary wisdom of great managers isn't. Their path is much more exacting. It demands discipline, focus, trust, and, perhaps most important, a willingness to individualize. In this book, great managers present no sweeping theories, no prefabricated formulae. All they can offer you are insights into the nature of talent and into their secrets for turning talent into performance. The real challenge lies in how you incorporate these insights into *your* style, one employee at a time, every day.[9]

The authors attempted to focus their investigation on what were the core values or *archai* of good management. What were the secrets to finding and keeping talented employees? By asking such questions, they deepened their understanding of organizational life. A questionnaire was developed that provided a snapshot of the organizational culture and at the same time linked the questions themselves to mainstream corporate concerns: profitability, productivity, employee turnover, and customer satisfaction. More importantly, the research indicated what the authors termed the "Four Keys" as core activities for management. They state that conventional wisdom in current organizational development produce these four maxims in *First, Break All the Rules*:

1. select a person…based on his experience, intelligence, and determination.

2. set expectations…by defining the right steps.

3. motivate the person…by helping him identify and overcome his weaknesses.

4. develop the person…by helping him learn and get promoted.

Instead of these traditional conclusions, the authors indicate that the insights common to great managers are:

1. *People don't change that much.*

2. *Don't waste time trying to put in what was left out.*

3. *Try to draw out what was left in.*

4. *That is hard enough.*[10]

Buckingham and Coffman conclude that the application of these insights to core activities result in the following methodology, termed the *Four Keys*:

1. when selecting someone, *they select for talent*...not simply experience, intelligence and determination.

2. when setting expectations, *they define the right outcomes*...not the right steps.

3. when motivating someone, *they focus on strengths*...not on weaknesses.

4. when developing someone, *they help him find the right fit*...not simply the next rung on the ladder.[11]

In particular, these four keys—natural talent, right outcomes, individual strengths and right fit—are a path to individuation, as the focus is on the development of the individual and his or her talents and subsequent performance; not on the corporation. Such an approach requires certainly more skill at a management level, but more importantly, Gallup indicates that such an approach can be correlated to greater profitability, productivity, employee retention, and customer satisfaction.

Marcus Buckingham and Donald O. Clifton built upon the initial research in *First, Break all the Rules,* and delivered a subsequent book, *Now, Discover Your Strengths,* published in 2001. As the title suggests, the book offers additional research on the importance of developing an individual's unique talent and strengths. Traditional organizational development focuses on employee weakness. Professional development has concentrated on deficiency training, while attempting to increase individual competency. Capitalizing on employee differences, the Gallup organization suggests the revolutionary idea of changing the way organizations select and measure employees in order to maximize individual strengths. Gallup asked the question: ""At work do you have the opportunity to do what you do best every day?" canvassing 198,000 employees working in 7,939 business units within 36 countries."[12] Gallup reported:

When employees answered, "strongly agree" to this question, they were 50 percent more likely to work in business units with lower employee turnover, 38 percent more likely to work in more productive business units, and 44 percent more likely to work in business units with higher customer satisfaction scores. And over time those business units that increased the number of employees who strongly agreed saw comparable increases in productivity, customer loyalty and employee retention. Whichever way you care to slice the data, the organization whose employees feel that their strengths are used every day is more powerful and robust.[13]

From an organizational perspective, the Gallup findings support the notion that employee development, or in archetypal terms, individuation, is perhaps the greatest source of potential for high-margin growth and shareholder value in organizations.

Gallup further suggests how such an approach could be implemented. First, discover an instrument for measuring talent to complement the selection process. Second, calibration of the instrument can be accomplished by studying the top performers in the organization. Third, instruct all managers in these concepts of finding and enhancing individual strengths. Fourth, build a thematic profile of the organization that will highlight necessary strengths.

One limitation of the Gallup research is that a process of implementation of these suggestions is missing from the work. Both books demonstrate a clear understanding of why professional development could and should be improved and potentially sustained in an organization. How that is accomplished requires further exploration.

Collins and Porras in *Built to Last* address some of these concerns of implementation. A comparison study was undertaken at Stanford Business School between what was termed "good companies and great companies." All of the companies in the research studied met the following criteria:

- Premier institution in its industry

- Widely admired by knowledgeable business people

- Made an indelible imprint on the world in which we live

- Had multiple generations of chief executives

- Been through multiple product (or service) life cycles

- Founded before 1950[14]

The researchers picked the organizations to be studied by initially sending questionnaires to the top executives in the United States asking each Chief Executive Officer (CEO) to nominate a "visionary company." After receiving responses, a comparison company was chosen in the same industry as the "visionary company" that had been nominated. The companies in the research study are listed below.

Visionary and Comparison Companies[15]

Visionary Companies Nominated	Comparison Company Selected
3M	Norton
American Express	Wells Fargo
Boeing	McDonnell Douglas
Citicorp	Chase Manhattan
Ford	GM
General Electric	Westinghouse
Hewlett-Packard	Texas Instruments
IBM	Burroughs
Johnson & Johnson	Bristol-Meyers Squibb
Marriott	Howard Johnson
Merck	Pfizer
Motorola	Zenith
Nordstrom	Melville
Philip Morris	RJR Nabisco
Proctor & Gamble	Colgate
Sony	Kenwood
Wal-Mart	Ames
Walt Disney	Columbia

Collins and Porras emphasized that both groups of companies were considered leaders in the field. Both groups were also publicly traded, which facilitated the collection of research data. The difference was that the "visionary companies" were exemplary and displayed a remarkable ability to recover from any adverse market conditions. The authors tracked stock prices over a sixty-four year period that indicated the resiliency of the "visionary companies" and reported:

> [...] visionary companies attain extraordinary *long-term* performance. Suppose you made equal $1 investments in a general-market stock fund, a comparison stock fund, and a visionary company stock fund on January 1, 1926. If you reinvested all dividends and made appropriate adjustments for when the com-

panies became available on the Stock Exchange (we held companies at general market rates until they appeared on the market), your $1 in the general market fund would have grown to $415 on December 31, 1990—not bad. Your $1 invested in the group of comparison companies would have grown to $955—more than twice the general market. But your $1 in the visionary companies stock fund would have grown to $6,356—over six times the comparison fund and over fifteen times the general market.[16]

The authors studied what the visionary companies did differently than the comparison companies and reported the following counterintuitive results. Well beyond identifying key strengths of employees that are underutilized as researched by the Gallup Organization, Collins and Porras found that a much deeper view must be taken to identify those characteristics that support a visionary company. The authors noted that an emphasis is not on the question "How should we change?" but rather on, "What do we stand for and why do we exist?" The last two questions are the foundation of the individuation process, to find what the authors termed a core ideology.

> In our advisory work we've been able to help multidisciplinary companies discover and articulate a unifying, global core ideology. In one company with operations in twenty-eight countries, most of the executives—a cynical and skeptical group—simply didn't believe it possible to find a shared set of core values and a common purpose that would be both global and meaningful. Through an intense process of introspection, beginning with each executive thinking about the core values he or she personally brings to his or her work, the group did indeed discover and articulate a shared core ideology.[17]

Although the core ideology and drive for progress usually trace their roots to specific individuals, a highly visionary company *institutionalizes* them—weaving them into the very fabric of the organization.[18]

> We've found that organizations often have great intentions and inspiring visions for themselves, but they don't take the crucial step of translating their intentions into concrete items. Even worse, they often tolerate organizational characteristics, strategies, and tactics that are misaligned with their admirable intentions, which creates confusion and cynicism. The gears and mechanisms of the ticking clock do not grind against each other but rather work in concert—in alignment with each other—to preserve the core and stimulate progress. The builders of visionary companies seek alignment in strategies, in tactics, in organizational systems, in structure, in incentive systems, in building layout, in job design—in everything.[19]

Further, in order to preserve the core and stimulate progress, a both/and approach must be taken that can accommodate this paradox. The authors emphasize the interplay between what they term "core ideology and the drive for progress"[20] as indicated below.

Interplay between Core Ideology and Drive for Progress

Core Ideology	Drive for Progress
Provides continuity and *stability*	Urges continual *change* (new directions, new methods, new strategies, and so on).
Plants a relatively *fixed* stake in the ground.	Impels constant *movement* (toward goals, improvement, an envisioned form, and so on).
Limits possibilities and directions for the company (to those consistent with the content of the ideology).	*Expands* the number and variety of possibilities that the company can consider.
Has clear content ("*This* is our core ideology and we will not breach it).	Can be content-free ("*Any* progress is good, as long as it is consistent with our core").
Installing a core ideology is, by its very nature, a *conservative* act.	Expressing the drive for progress can lead to dramatic, radical and *revolutionary* change.

A further elaboration on the usefulness of this construct from *Built to Last* will be explored in chapter 4, where post-Jungians James Hillman and Wolfgang Geigerich will be contrasted in their approach to working from an archetypal perspective that incorporates both sides of this apparent paradox.

Using An Archetypal Approach

The archetypal intersection points between corporate climate and the lens of leadership in the process of individuation are an alternative paradigm to the formulation of corporate strategy. It would be useful to the corporate world to bring an archetypal approach to the concept of "best practices" currently used in organizational development. The *mythos* emerging from the corporate sector encompasses moral as well as financial dimensions. After the crisis in confidence precipitated by the collapse of Enron and WorldCom in the United States, traditional values appear to be re-surfacing, and a close examination of these values provides a framework on which to build or renew organizations. More than a trendy indulgence, this emphasis on a defined and lived value system is an integral part of effective management. Today, the secret to winning the loyalty of professionals is understanding and responding to their shift in values. At the same time, fluid demographics demands the incorporation of a core value system capable of supporting both local and global perspectives, as well as a organic methodology capable of containing both old and new priorities. The use of an archetypal approach provides an insight into the ability to maintain this tension of the opposites, to work and grow in an environment of paradox.

Issues or Concerns Addressed
Using An Archetypal Model

An archetypal approach is a particularly apt solution to the rapid changes taking place in today's business for a variety of reasons. In *Kinds of Power*, James Hillman suggests: "[c]larification of the mind by attending to language is a method that begins with Confucius and with Socrates. Both held that the rectification of any problem begins with the careful consideration of speech."[21] An archetypal approach to organizational development is interdisciplinary and lends itself to the network of relationships required to maintain both a global and tribal perspective. This type of approach involves a polytheistic[22] *both/and* instead of a dualistic *either/or*. To view business from an archetypal lens encourages the perspectives of both local and global economies and ensures the primacy of relationship by such multiple views. The quality of an organization can be evaluated by viewing the quality of the inter-relationship among its employees without pathologizing these relationships.

Archetypal or depth psychology may infer a phenomenological view, allowing for a participatory process rather than a definitive result; it values experience over things. Perhaps with the emergence of the Internet into the business environment, a paradigm reducing the importance of space/time relationships has become necessary. An archetypal lens enables a shift toward a moral responsibility as well as an implied contract; a law above the law itself. Underscoring the value of the archetypal or "spirit" rather than the "letter" of the law creates room for an integrative vision to be found through relationship, recognition, and meaning.

A mission statement that remains on a wall of a corporation has no substance. It informs the reader of what is *claimed,* an "espoused value rather than values-in-action."[23] For a mission statement to be meaningful, it must come from a working belief system, a *mythos*. The adoption of a living *mythos* establishes and clarifies both espoused values and values-in-action and is demonstrated by daily-lived behavior. Such a mythos also has a component of story, or stories, that exemplify and communicate the actual operational values of the organization.

How to Use This Book

Chapters 2, 3 and 4 contain the theory that supports the integration of archetypal psychology and organizational development through the individuation process. For those readers who are not interested in the history and the 'why'—you may wish to skip these chapters. People are richly diverse in motivation and any attempt to simplify the complexity of human behaviour, contributes to the problems inherent in organizations today. There is no quick fix or instant solution. Building relationships takes time.

For those who follow the work of C.G. Jung, Chapter 2 expands the metamythology or motivational construct offered by Jung in his psychic drive theory to provide an overview of each stage of the construct in relation to organizational life. In addition, it incorporates the psychological discipline of archetypal psychology to help illuminate the substance of drive fulfillment on the path of individuation.

This working model will expand on Jung's theory. Such a metamythology is the foundation of tacit knowledge and that if such knowledge can be brought to consciousness, both individuals (knowledge workers) and the collective (the corporation) will benefit on their respective, yet shared, journeys toward individuation. Jung's metamythology is mapped using a visual model based on Campbell's Heroic Journey, which serves as a primary tool of integration.

A combination of both the theory and praxis is provided as a solution to the problem of tacit knowledge loss that accompanies a transient workforce. An archetypal or values-based approach is a vehicle that can contain the paradoxical aspects of knowledge management by bringing awareness to the "sub-stance," to what it is that *stands under* the current organizational theory. Archetypal theory can assist in materializing the seemingly intangible aspects of a corporate culture; the culture becomes newly visible, even to and especially to those responsible for creating it. Finally, an archetypal paradigm offers the possibility of an integration point between organizational and psychological theory that will better serve both communities.

Chapter 3 will outline the stages of the Heroic Journey Model as explored by Joseph Campbell. The Heroic Journey as an image or 'map' will represent both the process of psychological change and provide a framework by which to understand and guide such process. Due to the popularity in the lay public of the Heroic Journey, the map provides a familiar visual aid to guide the complex process of individuation.

Chapter 4 will outline how the work of C. G. Jung and Joseph Campbell can be expanded and integrated in an organizational setting. Campbell, especially through his work on the Heroic Journey, provides an image as a visual representation of the process of change. The psychological drive theory, as presented by Jung, can be used as a guideline for the psychological process necessary for change to occur. The work of James Hillman and Wolfgang Geigerich will be explored in order to show the compensatory aspects of the intersection between actual (image) and potential (thought).

Readers who wish to skip the theory should start at Chapter 5—Preparation for the Journey. You can always return later to the psychological underpinnings when you wish to learn more about the theory.

Chapter 6 will expand on the first aspect of the Heroic Journey—The Call. This chapter will be supported with examples from current cultural practices in organizations. A section on praxis will draw parallels between aspects of psychic hunger and the belief systems of knowledge workers and how these create and impact the structure of a corporation. The psychic value of hunger is that it propels the individual toward an undefined goal; in other words it is the beginning place of the Journey—The Call.

Chapter 7 will focus on the second aspect of the Heroic Journey—Initiation. Initiation is a now undervalued component of the life cycle and is useful in defining roles, whether personal or organizational. If the physical senses are viewed as allies within, then intuitive knowing can be differentiated from logical knowing. Without diminishing the value of either sense, aspects of initiation introduce how both forms of knowing are invaluable in further growth. The section on praxis will show how the use of an educational program served to initiate employees into a newly formed approach to create generative and sustainable leadership.

Chapter 8 will focus on the third component of the Heroic Journey—that of the Ordeal. This parallels Jung's drive of activity. The section on praxis will include the paralleling of ordeals of corporate life and the translation of values into personal and corporate behavior. Productive activity within an organization comes from establishing common core values and gathering community and storytelling holds the potential to render tacit knowledge explicit, thus increasing awareness or consciousness.

Chapter 9 will examine the fourth aspect of the Heroic Journey, that of Breakthrough and parallels Jung's drive of reflection. The section on praxis will include parallels with the level of commitment to open communication within the corporation itself, and examine the spirit of meeting one's calling, taking one's place in the world and leaving a legacy of meaning. The importance of memory will also be explored as the source of energy that transforms an "event" into an experience.

Chapter 10 will focus on the final aspect of the Heroic Journey, Celebration, and parallels Jung's psychological drive of creativity. The section on praxis will focus on the use of creative process in personal and organizational life and how such process defines the purpose of the journey itself.

Chapter 11, "Re-Visioning" brings a fresh perspective on Jung's psychological constructs through the practical aspects of the Heroic Journey, particularly in the area of corporate culture. As a means of facing the challenges of a shrinking workforce and economic globalization, the integration of a reflective consciousness of one's individual myth with that of an organization or collective myth provides a relational framework through which both individuals and corporations can realize their creative potential. Archetypal psychology is grounded in multiplicity, which provides necessary flexibility in an organization. The parallels between Jung's metamythology and Campbell's visual representation of the Heroic Journey can be used as a further guide to provide working metaphors for a shifting structure in a global environment.

Notes—Introduction:

1. James Hillman, Kinds of Power, 16. This book is an excellent reference guide to the psychological use of power structures in organizations and the impact of having (or not having) power on people.

2. Ronald Heifetz, Leadership Without Easy Answers, 121. Heifetz is one of the few organizational theorists who had the courage to stay with the complexity inherent in dealing with people. This is an excellent reference on leadership.

3. James Hillman, Kinds of Power, 31. Many refer to James Hillman, along with David Miller, as the founders of Archetypal Psychology, the next wave of work from those who are direct students of C.G. Jung. An introduction to the work of James Hillman is "The Soul's Code" which became a best-seller.

4. Ibid, 102.

5. Campbell, Hero of a Thousand Faces, 16. This is the book that George Lucas used as a foundation for Star Wars. An excellent introduction to mythology. See also the popular PBS Special with Bill Moyers, "The Power of Myth" to see Campbell in action.

6. Jung, CW8: 246.

7. Hillman, Myth of Analysis, 7.

8. Hillman, Kinds of Power, 51.

9. Buckingham and Coffman, First Break All the Rules, 12. This is an excellent resource book for examining and/or exploring your corporate culture. This book contains the Q12 questionnaire, which has become a popular measurement of organizational culture. The authors and the Gallup Organization have linked ROI (return on investment) directly to specific cultural conditions such as employee retention, customer satisfaction, productivity and profitability. Easy to read and easy to use.

10. Ibid, 66.

11. Ibid, 67.

12. Ibid, 5.

13. Buckingham and Clifton, Now, Discover Your Strengths, 6. This is the follow-up book to "First, Break All the Rules." An excellent resource for the argument of managing by people's inherent strengths rather than attempting to "fix" weakness although provides an interesting management problem of putting people together like pieces of a puzzle. The Strengthsfinder questionnaire can be taken on-line and a printout of your top five strengths will be returned. An interesting experience in itself!

14. Collins and Porras, Built to Last, 2. This bestseller was researched and written while Jim Collins taught the "Creativity in Business" program with Michael Ray at the Stanford Graduate School of Business. An excellent guide to what made various highly successful public companies sustainable over time. Further research needs to be done in this area to see if these principles can translate into private profit and non-profit organizations. My guess would be yes.

15. Ibid, 3.

16. Ibid, 4.

17. Ibid, xvii.

18. Ibid, 86.

19. Ibid, 87.

20. Ibid, 85.

21. Hillman, Kinds of Power, 12.

22. See "The New Polytheism" by David Miller. Miller is also credited with helping to found archetypal psychology and this work is exceptional in exploring the use of a multiple lens by which to view our world.

23. Edgar Schein, Organizational Culture and Leadership, 1992. This book should be considered a classic in organizational theory. Schein originally coined the terms 'espoused values' and 'values-in-action' and his exploration of the difference and potential disconnects between the two are worth examining.

The Metamythology Of C. G. Jung

In 1936, C. G. Jung presented an essay at Harvard University entitled "Psychological Factors Determining Human Behavior." His short essay is the foundation of my work and the starting point for my own opus. Jung suggests that a Psyche/body split is artificial, that "psyche is absolutely identical to the state of being alive."[1] Psyche can be examined from both a personal and organizational perspective that addresses the growing problem of inert organizations and a consequent demoralization in the corporate workforce. Jung's work is renowned for its complexity and inaccessibility. Applying it to the corporate milieu of balance sheets and bottom lines is admittedly challenging. It my goal to provide a link between the work or opus of the individual and that of C. G. Jung's individuation, using the Hero's Journey articulated by Joseph Campbell as the mythological bridge between two seemingly disparate worlds: psychology and business.

To engage in scholarly research that is truly innovative can be daunting. Breaking new ground is, by definition, risky, but it is the focus and goal of many scholars. The question remains: *how can the balance between scholarship and innovation be achieved?* Archetypal psychology, with its blend of traditional and innovative components, provides one possible solution. The archetypal realm is sufficiently multifaceted to handle the complexity of organizational theory and to bring that complexity to consciousness. As James Hillman claims:

> We are traditional because we return all things to their deepest principles, the *archai*, the limiting roots holding down and in. They determine by recurring with fatalistic regularity, little caring for place or time. We are revolutionary because these same *archai* are the radicals of existence. They will out, always. They force the claims of the dispossessed soul upon the ruling consciousness of each place and time.[2]

Management at any organizational level can be guided in "seeing through" an organization's own mythology, the current ruling consciousness of corporate existence. The foundation of such a mythology is in the *archai,* those aspects of organizational self, the collective that provides the cultural components to its existence. Just as DNA provides the building blocks of physical reality, it is axiomatic that archetypes found psychic reality. As Hillman further claims:

> Here I am positing patterns of power in the imagination, patterns prior to ideas and revealed in the ideas. These are *archai*, the Greek term for root principles, the basic metaphors on which all things rest and which give consistently typical forms and styles of expression to the way we think, feel and talk.[3]

A corporate mythology based on a corporation's *archai* is defined as "who you are, and what you do" as opposed to a mission statement, which defines "what you *should be* doing." A corporate mythology is a fundamental pattern of ideas that may be brought to consciousness in order to function as the driving force of an organization. It is the organization's continuing source of power and the engine that drives future sustainable growth.

Uncovering the Myths of an Organization

Hillman defines the task of psychology as "the care and service of the ill Psyche."[4] I regard the task of the archetypal psychologist as the care and service of the healthy psyche, or in corporate life, the care of the soul of the organization. In order to care for the psyche adequately, the contextual framework of an individual or organization must be considered. Logic is limited to what we already know; to reach beyond it and to innovate requires access to another realm of knowledge. Late in his life, Jung observes in *Memories, Dreams, Reflections* "the more critical reason dominates, the more impoverished life becomes; but the more of the unconscious, and the more of myth we are capable of making conscious, the more of life we integrate."[5] In an organizational context, this statement means the realization that innovation and creativity stem from unexpected or unplanned acts. The creativity process cannot be forced or mandated into existence. If an organization creates and nurtures an environment whereby acts of creativity can 'happen' rather than be orchestrated, such an environment will also support an interplay between what is known and what is potentially possible. These two states, in Jungian terms, are called the conscious mind or ego (being what is known) and the unconscious (being unknown, a state of pure potential).

Research conducted by Jung and the post-Jungians provides a framework by which such integration is possible through the individuation process. Very little attention has been given to the application of Jungian psychology to organizational life. To bring the power of myth, which is a language of imagination, to the workplace will be difficult. My experience leads me to believe that a conscious use of the mythic imagination is the key to this challenge, whereas the traditional language of both psychology and organizational theory has tended to pathologize individual and organizational behavior. Organizationally, this pathologizing amounts to a simplistic mindset of objective problem solving, which tends to avoid the entire depth psychological domain. Every success has a beginning, and that beginning is in the imagination, the home of creativity and innovation. To tell the stories of these beginnings and the journey to success is the function of corporate and individual myth. To bring such a mythic stance into day-to-day organizational life, is to revitalize the workplace as the human race has always been energized by story.

Physics has taught us that the observer affects what is observed, that energy takes form through the very act of observation.[6] Quantum theory suggests that energy is contained as *potential* in a nondualistic, *both/and* space. If location is observed or measured, energy becomes a particle, and if speed is observed or measured, energy becomes a wave. But energy, in its primary state, is both a particle and a wave, a concept difficult to grasp using traditional dualistic modes of thought. Physicist Niels Bohr was known to comment that those who are not shocked when they first come across quantum theory cannot possibly have understood it. According to the laws of physics, a new paradigm is needed, one that allows for *potential* to exist as a state of ambiguity without pathologizing it. Although perhaps shocking to traditional modes of thought, a mythic perspective encourages that potential, or mystery, back into perspective, to allow space for pure potential to be incorporated and included. According to Hillman:

> [...] if consciousness changes, then the neurosis that we have known as its counterpart will also come to an end, and so will analysis, which came into existence as an answer to neurosis. If, with insights, we penetrate analysis through to its mythical foundations, it collapses upon its three fallen pillars—transference, the unconscious, and neurosis—which we prefer to call, in accordance with the mythical perspective, the erotic, the imaginal, and the Dionysian.[7]

Hillman and other post-Jungians suggest that such a change in consciousness can be brought about by a penetration of analysis into a mythical perspective and that this strategy is the foundation of archetypal psychology. As Hillman states, this perspective includes "the erotic, the imaginal and the Dionysian." Such a mythical approach may incorporate the use of image and storytelling to expand conscious awareness.

Psychological Modalities

In order to create space for such a mythical perspective, Jung speaks of three psychological modalities.[8] The first modality is an individual's consciousness, the degree to which action and thought are formulated from a conscious or unconscious viewpoint. The second psychological modality is an individual's mode of perception, or awareness, which categorizes an individual as extroverted or introverted. The third modality, again dealing with an individual's sensory acuity, concerns whether perception occurs largely through matter or spirit, through the body or through the mind. The first modality of consciousness is of particular interest here since it can be specifically applied to the study of tacit knowledge within corporate organizations.

Conscious/Unconscious

Directly accessing any unconscious content—individual or corporate—is impossible, but the mythology or story of an organization is accessible, and therefore provides entry into decoding that world. The role of an archetypal psychologist is to help bring this mythology to conscious awareness. To look at the internal structure of any organization requires a depth psychological approach since it is the "sub-stance" of an organization that drives the whole. In the concrete world of organizations, introducing the abstract notion of consciousness is admittedly challenging. Jung claims, however, that "consciousness is primarily an organ of orientation in a world of outer and inner facts."[9] In order to make use of this *organ,* the inner state of being must be acknowledged as at least relevant, if not paramount to psychic health. In terms of corporate culture, it must be understood that to remain unaware of the manifestations of the corporate unconscious is perilous to the psychological health of an organization.

> Experience in analytical psychology has amply shown that the conscious and the unconscious seldom agree as to their contents and their tendencies. This lack of parallelism is not just accidental or purposeless, but is due to the fact that the unconscious behaves in a compensatory or complementary manner towards the conscious.[10]

Jung maintains that compensation occurs when the unconscious attempts to bring another aspect into the realm of consciousness. If the current state of organizations necessitated government intervention to ensure compliance with laws to protect both individuals and corporations, then current economic forces have become too one-sided. Such a position, according to Jung, will force a compensatory response and may offer an explanation why intervention was required. As Jung warns, "[…] those people who are least aware of their unconscious side are the most influenced by it. But they are unconscious of what is happening."[11] To assist in bringing a corporate mythos to consciousness, another modality may provide additional insight.

Extrovert/Introvert

This modality forms the part of the foundation of what Jung refers to as the Psychology of Types. A detailed examination of this work is beyond the scope of this book, although the extrovert/introvert modality provides the impetus for energy to be directed either externally from or internally, to the individual. This energy flow will be explored as a method of problem solving in practice. Jung elaborates further:

> It determines the direction of psychic activity, that is, it decides whether the conscious contents refer to external objects or to the subject. Therefore, it also decides whether the value stressed lies outside or inside the individual. This modality operates so persistently that it builds up habitual attitudes, that is, types with recognizable outward traits.[12]

"Locus of control" refers to whether the individual is moved by internal or external forces. In *Aion: Researches into the Phenomenology of the Self*, Jung explores how the impetus for locus of control can affect the field of personal awareness of consciousness.

> Theoretically, no limits can be set to the field of consciousness, since it is capable of indefinite extension. Empirically, however, it always finds its limit when it comes up against the *unknown*. This consists of everything we do not know, which, therefore, is not related to the ego as the center of the field of consciousness. The unknown falls into two groups of objects: those which are outside and can be experienced by the senses, and those which are inside and are experienced immediately. The first group comprises the unknown in the outer world; the second the unknown in the inner world.[13]

Locus of control directly affects decision-making and problem solving, the span of which affects each of five psychological aspects described by Jung. The complexity of this strategy is not to be underestimated, as Hillman cautions:

> Introversion never meant isolation from the human community. Introversion is an attitude, a description of energy flow, and not the precondition for soul-making; it must be carefully distinguished in theory and in actuality from the opus.[14]

Locus of control may also assist in the manifestation of tacit knowledge when an individual is motivated by either internal or external factors. Regardless of what psychological type is dominant, each type has a theoretical and practical component. Organizationally, this might be seen as whether an individual gathers energy for innovation by primarily self-reflection (introversion) or whether energy is gathered from stimulation from other people (extroversion).

Psyche/Soma

Jung stresses the "enormous challenge of integrating psyche and soma" in the process of individuation.[15] If each life can be viewed from a mythic perspective, it is possible to achieve a physical experience of imagination, linking passion to action in order to create a way of being with others. Jung argues that such integration is in constant need of examination. Of this modality, he explains:

> The third modality points, to use a metaphor, upward and downward, because it has to do with spirit and matter. It is true that matter is in general the subject of physics, but it is also a psychic category, as the history of religion and philosophy clearly shows. And just as matter is ultimately to be conceived of merely as a working hypothesis of physics, so also is spirit, the subject of religion and philosophy, is a hypothetical category in constant need of reinterpretation.[16]

Applied research can serve as a system through which theory and practice reinforce each other. This book extends beyond existing research to explore how both individuals *and* organizations self-actualize or individuate. It is informed largely by Hillman's observation that "there shall be no definition, which limits and cuts, but rather amplification, which extends and connects."[17] Through the language of mythology, the public realm of business can be linked with the private domain of the individual using Jung's psychological modalities of Conscious and Unconscious, Inward and Outward, and Psyche and Soma.

The Transcendent Function

Jung's theories are based on his clients' and his own transformative experiences; and the extensive body of work that has resulted largely from Jung's personal psychological journey has yet to be fully explored. His concept of Wholeness, or of the Self, is not only an intellectual one; it needs to be understood experientially. The development of awareness, or consciousness, is gradual and ultimately leads to *individuation*, Jung's term for the process that is undertaken usually in the second half of life. *Life is an experience—not a theory.*

Often this process is mistaken as selfishness, or even narcissism, but nothing could be further from Jung's intention:

> The unrelated human being lacks wholeness, for he can achieve wholeness only through the soul, and the soul cannot exist without its other side, which is always found in a "You." Wholeness is a combination of I and You and these show themselves to be parts of a transcendent unity whose nature can only be grasped symbolically.[18]

This dialectic, the dialogue between the "I and You" is frequently expressed through story. As such, the story re-tells the experience of a confrontation with the unconscious. A story returns us to the imaginal, creating a sacred space, a *temenos*, which contains the experience. Jung reminds us, however, "life has always to be tackled anew."[19] To re-member is to re-create, to give body to the experience once again, thus continuing a process of a sort of circumambulation or deeply circling that Jung claims is fundamental to the understanding of the encounter. To circle the story in the re-telling takes one deeper and deeper into the potential for transformation. According to Jung, "if a life-mass is to be transformed, a *circumambulatio* must be reached, namely an exclusive concentration on the center, the place of creative change."[20] The *circumambulatio* is the center of individual experience, where opposites meet and conflict, where two opposing views or two divergent paths present themselves as circumstances beyond individual control. Jung observed, "It is not I who create myself, rather I happen to myself."[21]

The *circumambulatio* is a testing ground. As Jung notes: "The self is made manifest in the opposites and in the conflict between them. [...] Hence the way to the self begins with conflict."[22] St. John of the Cross aptly referred to this place of conflict and potential transformation as the *dark night of the soul,* where crisis must be endured and accepted until clarity is restored. Jung cautions that this often entails an almost unbearable tension because of the utter incommensurability between conscious life and the unconscious process, which can be experienced only in the innermost soul and cannot touch the visible surface of life at any point. [23]

Out of such crisis comes what Jung labels a "transcendent function," or third thing, the mystery that provides the answer and the resulting expansion of consciousness. Hillman elaborates on Jung's approach to the creative:

> Where he does turn to the creative instinct as such, his descriptions are given under other conceptions of it: the urge to wholeness, the urge toward individuation or personality development, the spiritual drive, the symbol-making transcendent function, the natural religious function, or in short, the drive of the self to be realized. He strongly affirms that this urge to self-realization works with the compulsiveness of an instinct. We are driven to be ourselves.[24]

In this sense, the transcendent function is the foundation on which storytelling rests, the home of expression that is mythopoetic in nature. It is through this ongoing process that "we are driven to be ourselves."

Jung claims that the transcendent function arises from the union of conscious and unconscious contents."[25] It is a balance point between the two opposites, the two extremes that hold a person immobile. To an objection that some conflicts are insoluble, Jung replies:

> People sometimes take this view because they think only of external solutions—which at bottom are not solutions at all. [...] A real solution comes only from within, and then only because the patient has been brought to a different attitude.[26]

In other words, the answer lies inside of us. Whether actual solution or an increased level of consciousness, through the lens of the transcendent function a story can become a *temenos,* a sacred space that enables a single voice to give expression to two extremes. It creates thereby a dialetic that gives voice to each extreme without negating the "other." Individuation demands the holding of such tension since relating to others first requires a relationship with the Self. Jung adds:

> From the activity of the unconscious there now emerges a new content, constellated by thesis and antithesis in equal measure and standing in *compensa-*

tory relationship to both. It thus forms the middle ground on which the opposites can be united.[27]

Such union can be transmitted outwardly and reinforced inwardly by communicating the experience of the meeting of unconscious and conscious contents in the *temenos* of a story. A personal story is enfolded within the world story, which is wrapped around the personal story. The interaction, the dynamic play between the two stories, creates a transcendent third that incorporates both. The story holds the intensity of emotion until transformed into experience. The experience is then communicated again through story. As such, story can be the basis of forming or deepening relationships based on shared communication.

Myth provides a shared language that describes a relationship to the Self, to others, to society and to the cosmos in a given context. Myth is viewed as a primordial language natural to psychic processes; it could be argued that intellectual formulation does not come near to the richness and expressiveness of mythical imagery. Jung spoke in terms of primordial images, and these "are best and most succinctly reproduced by figurative language."[28] As such, these images provide the rationale for the working language of story. The continuing story that is lived and told sets an individual apart from day-to-day existence, a personal reality, and provides instead a context that allows space for the mystery to enter. As Jungian analyst D. Stephenson Bond observes: "In the encounter with the 'Not-I', as the alien within, the collective unconscious becomes not an idea, but a relationship."[29] In an anonymous letter of condolence in 1947, Jung claimed, "life is a luminous pause between two great mysteries which yet are one.[30] When stories are exchanged, a space is made for these mysteries, for what is not yet understood. In reciting a story, an unspoken invitation is extended to the listener to make comment, provide insight, and thus enable further exploration of the mystery waiting just beyond the story itself.

Jung and many post-Jungian psychologists argue that myth is the language of the psyche. In addition, psyche speaks in images, pictures, stories—all of which are larger than a single life. Myth provides a map of psyche that gives expression and meaning to the events of an individual's life. Through mythic themes, a language of meaning can be rediscovered, the focus of one's life work, according to Jung:

> The need for mythic statements is satisfied when we frame a view of the world which adequately explains the meaning of human existence in the cosmos, a view which springs from our psychic wholeness, from the cooperation between conscious and unconscious. Meaninglessness inhibits fullness of life

and is therefore equivalent to illness. Meaning makes a great many things endurable—perhaps everything. [31]

The transcendent function can be accessed through dreams and through fantasy, to allow for a potential dialogue between the unconscious and consciousness. If the psyche is viewed as an energy system that strives for balance, then should the conscious mind become too one-sided, the unconscious will attempt to compensate for the imbalance. As Jung explains:

> Civilized life today demands concentrated, directed conscious functioning, and this entails the risk of a considerable dissociation from the unconscious. The further we are able to remove ourselves from the unconscious through directed functioning, the more readily a powerful counter-position can build up in the unconscious, and when this breaks out it may have disagreeable consequences. [32]

Psyche is a system of *both/and*, not one of *either/or*. It is the ego that differentiates, that orders in a dualistic fashion, whereas the psyche is a system of paradox, holding opposites in a unified space, allowing the potential realization of *both*. One of the tasks of individuation is to deepen the relationship with the unconscious permitting awareness of the significance in compensatory relationship. As Jung states: "it makes the transition from one attitude to another organically possible, without loss of the unconscious."[33]

Jung suggests two methods of processing material produced by these compensatory dreams and fantasies. One is through creative formulation and the other is the way of understanding. It is possible to consider the way of understanding as abstraction, pure thought or the meaning-making aspects of memory and recollection and the way of creative formulation to be any creative act. With such a method, two aspects materialize:

> Where the principle of creative formulation predominates, the material is continually varied and increased until a kind of condensation of motifs into more or less stereotyped symbols takes place. These stimulate the creative fantasy and serve chiefly as aesthetic motifs. This tendency leads to the aesthetic problem of artistic formulation.[34]

And the second aspect:

> Where, on the other hand, the principle of understanding predominates, the aesthetic aspect is of relatively little interest and may occasionally even be felt

as a hindrance. Instead, there is an intensive struggle to understand the *meaning* of the unconscious product. [35]

Jung states that "*one tendency seems to be the regulating principle of the other,* both are bound together in a compensatory relationship."[36] Again, according to Jung, both are needed to transcend the conflict of the opposites:

> So far as it is possible at this stage to draw more general conclusions, we could say that aesthetic formulation needs understanding of the meaning, and understanding need aesthetic formulation. The two supplement each other to form the transcendent function.[37]

In organizations this function can occur through telling and retelling the mythic stories that reside in the collective conscious and unconscious of its members. The telling of those stories activates this transcendent function, the empirical result of which is the organizing process that creates what is referred to as "an organization," as if it were a static thing. In reality, we understand that it comes into being and slips out again as mythic stories are told, enacted, and forgotten, only to start the cycle of telling again.

The Transcendent Function and Relationship

When I listen to the story of a life, I listen for a hint of the transcendent function, for psyche always attempts to speak. By looking at how relationship is created by the individual, either to Self or to Other, a path to further understanding or increased consciousness deepens. By re-membering and so embodying the story, the experience is re-lived. If an individual were to use Jung's method of amplification of the story by giving attention to the symbols that arise, then a deepening of the story may be experienced by the individual, which allows potentially different outcomes. Jung considers this act of re-membering or memory to be an *endopsychic* function. To illustrate, an endopsychic function is a system of relationship between conscious contents and unconscious processes. As such "the function of memory, or reproduction, links us up with things that have faded out of consciousness, things that became subliminal or were cast away or repressed."[38]

To tell a story provides some measure of objectivity by removing oneself slightly from the intimacy of the experience. This distance is sometimes all that is needed for unconscious contents to break through into consciousness. This process Jung terms *invasion* and also considers it a function of endopsychic processes by which the unconscious could break into the conscious condition.[39] In each re-telling of a story, the possibility for such breakthrough exists, and Jung considers there to be no difference between "artistic inspiration and invasion."[40]

The story may be retold initially to the Self, but it also may be told to an Other, and in the re-telling creates relationship. If the exchange remains superficial, then the individual may remain "stuck" in a repetition compulsion. The meaning of the story does not change. If a space is created whereby unconscious material can break through, the relationship is deepened by unconscious material becoming conscious. In this case, the meaning is altered by the deepening process.

Jung's views on this process were explicit:

> The self *is* relatedness; the self doesn't exist without relationship. Only when the self mirrors itself in so many mirrors does it really exist—then it has roots. You can never come to yourself by building a meditation hut on top of Mount Everest; you will only be visited by your own ghosts and that is not individuation: you are all alone with yourself and *the* self doesn't exist. [...] Not that you *are,* but that you *do* is the self. The self appears in your deeds, and deeds always mean relationship.[41]

The Transcendent Function and Recognition

Through the *temenos* of story an individual is able to hold the tension of opposites and potentially create a form of dialogue, whether internal or external, to allow an exchange between conscious and unconscious content. In other words, the quality of all relationships stems from the relationship to the Self. This recognition that the knowledge of the ego is limited to what is already known permits the comprehension at a deeper level, that only beyond the ego can further meaning be obtained.

> Once the unconscious content has been given form and the meaning of the formulation is understood, the question arises as to how the ego will relate to this position, and how the ego and the unconscious are to come to terms. This is the second and more important stage of the procedure, the bringing together of opposites for the production of a third: the transcendent function. At this stage it is no longer the unconscious that takes the lead, but the ego.[42]

Said in a different way, once unconscious material has been given some form, whether by artistic formulation or by ascribed meaning, the ego once more can predominate until such time when unconscious material again breaks through ego defenses. In order to improve our relationship with others, we must recognize rendering consciously the relationship with Self.

The myth being lived by the individual will hold the implicit value system of the individual. To recognize these implicit values is to bring the myth to conscious awareness. By an act of recognition, such motifs or clusters of motifs can be explored both by the individual and then by others in an organizational context. At this point, the psyche is arguably no longer something *within* but rather something in which the individual is contained.

The Transcendent Function and Meaning

Recognizing that each story, each life, has many such experiences of meaning makes possible the potential to coexist with fear of the unknown. Stories tell tales that stretch people because they give voice to the growth of the soul. Through the experience of story, a person can come into his or her own sense of body, and become the source of a developing understanding. Jung describes this experience as our natural tendency towards wholeness, a basic impulse towards unity in the psyche. For Jung, energy will always move towards the center of the circle, his symbol of wholeness. Beginning with one story, the path toward understanding the power and importance of all stories is forged and potentiality on every level is created. Jung notes that "change must begin with one individual; it might be any one of us."[43] Transformation of society, therefore, must begin with the transformation of the individual, the process of individuation which "does not shut one out from the world, but gathers the world to itself."[44]

A creative act is not just produced by the brilliant "other" unknown to the Self. Jung offers the following prediction:

> I do not wish to pass myself off as a prophet, but I cannot outline the spiritual problem of modern man without giving emphasis to the yearning for rest that arises in a period of unrest, or to the longing for security that is bred of insecurity. It is from need and distress that new forms of life take their rise, and not from mere wishes or from the requirements of our ideals.[45]

Organizational life and what it entails has forever been changed by the crisis of September 11, 2001. People in North America have reached a degree of uncertainty never before experienced. Faith in America's economic system has been shaken, perhaps deservedly so. Need and distress may provide an opportunity to create a new economic system that is more equitable, more capable of serving both the organization and the individual, both from local and global perspectives.

It is common, after September 11, 2001, to speak about that event as a ratio-nale for changes in corporate travel policy, or even individual travel preferences which may actually have nothing to do with the actual event. No matter, the event is mythically tied to the corporate and individual psyche, so it will emerge in the stories that are told.

Psychological distress, or the tension of the opposites, can be carried through the vehicle of story and communicated at a level deep enough in the psyche to demand change. Through such rites emerge tales of loss and love, sorrow and joy, birth and death, which we collect as a common history. These paradoxical rites of passage belong to the human race. They provide meaning for individuals and organizations. Jung observed that a neurosis "must be understood, ultimately, as the suffering of a soul which has not discovered its meaning."[46] Multiplicity of meanings can be intensified and explored through the metamythology Jung orig-inally formulated. These aspects can then be utilized as a methodology for creat-ing stories that transform both the economic climate and the psyche.

Importance of Relationship, Recognition, and Meaning in Organizational Life

In an organizational setting, the Gallup Organization has found that an employee doesn't leave a corporation; he or she leaves a manager, making the relationship between manager and knowledge worker of primary importance. In *First, Break All the Rules,* Buckingham and Coffman comment that "so much money has been thrown at the challenge of keeping good people—in the form of better pay, better perks, and better training—when, in the end, turnover is mostly a manager issue."[47] Of the twelve questions asked by the Gallup Questionnaire, "the most powerful questions are those with a combination of the strongest links to the *most* business outcomes." The following were found to be the most powerful ques-tions:

1. Do I know what is expected of me at work?

2. Do I have the materials and equipment I need to do my work right?

3. Do I have the opportunity to do what I do best every day?

4. In the last seven days, have I received recognition or praise for good work?

5. Does my supervisor, or someone at work, seem to care about me as a person?

6.   Is there someone at work who encourages my development?[48]

The important business outcomes were defined as "higher levels of productivity, profit, retention and customer satisfaction."[49] In archetypal terms, the first two of these questions would appear to be only indirectly linked to the process of individuation; they would support but not necessarily cause it. Alternatively, questions 3 through 6 directly link to the need for relationship, recognition, and meaning. Although it is but a superficial view, and much further research could and will be done, it would appear that the process of individuation, if undertaken by each worker and consciously supported by organizational leaders, would directly connect to positive business outcomes. In *Now, Discover Your Strengths* Buckingham and Clifton report that:

> [...] most organizations remain startlingly inefficient at capitalizing on the strengths of their people. In Gallup's total database we have asked the "opportunity to do what I do best" question of more than 1.7 million employees in 101 companies from 63 countries. What percentage do you think strongly agrees that they have an opportunity to do what they do best every day? What percentage truly feels that their strengths are in play? *Twenty percent.* [50]

Herein may lay the answer to a sluggish economy, weak performance, employee dissatisfaction, and many other organizational ills. If people, and therefore our organizations, are functioning at only 20% capacity, what can be done to engage the remaining 80% in each individual? I return again to the work of C. G. Jung.

Five Aspects of Instinctive Factors

Jung theorizes that "from a psychological standpoint five main groups of instinctive factors can be distinguished: hunger, sexuality, activity, reflection and creativity. In the last analysis, instincts are ectopsychic determinants."[51] I will briefly describe each of these aspects to provide the starting point as conceived by Jung; they will be expanded and amplified throughout this book.

Hunger. A question I frequently ask in my organizational consulting practice never fails to initiate a passionate discussion. The question is "What do you hunger for that you cannot name?" Regardless of at what level of organizational hierarchy, it would appear that employees immediately recognize their personal underutilization by management. An individual's potential is much, much greater than any job description. Thus, I use the analogy of *hunger* as an aspect of psychological reality. If each individual does hunger for relationship, recognition, and meaning, and if more than half of life is spent engaged in some kind of work, then it is a reasonable expectation to find satisfaction of this hunger in professional as well as personal life. I make no distinction between the two areas, for if an individual is fully engaged on a professional level, she or he will also be engaged at a personal level. Aspects of the transcendent function may be applicable in this case, since personal life and professional life usually are considered separate entities. Using an archetypal approach, one can observe how each aspect can inform the other to create a third. Jung comments on the distinctions between psychic hunger and physical hunger:

> No matter how unequivocal the physical state of excitation called hunger may be, the psychic consequences resulting from it can be manifold. Not only can the reactions to ordinary hunger vary widely, but the hunger itself can be "denatured," and can even appear as something metaphorical.[52]

If hunger is used as a metaphor to describe a deep desire for relationship, recognition, and meaning, and if that metaphor is explored in an organizational context, a different relationship to Self and the organization begins to emerge. Jung suggests that

> it is not only that we use the word hunger in different senses, but in combination with other factors hunger can assume the most varied forms. The originally simple and unequivocal determinant can appear transformed into pure greed, or into many aspects of boundless desire or insatiability, as for instance the lust for gain or inordinate ambition.[53]

It is self-evident from corporate scandals over the past few years that hunger, as an archetype of transformation, has a multiplicity of meanings. How metaphorical hunger has been utilized for organizational transformation will be explored in later chapters.

Sexuality. I will explore sexuality in terms of its generative function in an organizational context. Complexity is certainly a part of this aspect since sexuality can manifest in many different ways. Jung believes that

> the sexual instinct enters into combination with many different feelings, emotions, affects, with spiritual and material interests, to such a degree that, as is well known, the attempt has been made to trace the whole of culture to these combinations.[54]

Generativity as a function of leadership has spiritual roots. To explore generativity in the context of organizational life, individuation becomes a necessary component. If a leader can walk the difficult path of individuation, by the process itself the leader encourages others, by example, to find their own particular paths. When an individual is generative, the cycle of renewal is modeled for those that follow. Much has been written about leadership, but it is this overlooked aspect of generativity that stimulates growth. Individuation always takes place in relationship: to Self and to Other.

Activity. Jung's third aspect, activity, is the concretization of thought, or the impulse to action, and as such, is present in both individuals and organizations. *Knowledge plus action is power.* Activity is the means of satisfying or implementing other psychological aspects. Jung explains:

> I should like, then, to differentiate as a third group of instincts the *drive to activity*. This urge starts functioning when the other urges are satisfied; indeed, it is perhaps only called into being after this has occurred. Under this heading would come the urge to travel, love of change, restlessness, and the play-instinct.[55]

Activity might also be understood as the ability to solve problems in both personal and organizational spheres. The more an individual can align his or her world of conscious choice through applied core values with this drive to activity, the more the individual will be in harmony with the indications of the unconscious.

Reflection. Jung claims "as long as we are caught up in the process of creation, we neither see nor understand; indeed we ought not to understand, for nothing is more injurious to immediate experience than cognition."[56] However, in order for an event to become an experience and to be recognized as such, reflecting on the event is crucial to the process. Jung observes:

> Through the reflective instinct, the stimulus is more or less wholly transformed into a psychic content, that is, it becomes an experience: a natural process is transformed into a conscious content. Reflection is the culture instinct *par excellence*, and its strength is shown in the power of culture to maintain itself in the face of untamed nature.[57]

Again, in order to change an individual or an organization, mythology provides an approach for transformation. The emerging theme is that the process of managing change is a complex iteration, one best accomplished through multiple strategies. Such multiplicity can be found in archetypal psychology. By reflecting, an individual has the potential to engage deeply with whatever questions arise with a consequent opportunity to deepen relationship with Self and Other. Reflection enables one to discern the movement of the invisible, the mystery just beyond ego consciousness. Reflection invites invasion, or what Jung terms a breakthrough of unconscious content. Reflection creates a space whereby the transcendent function may appear through artistic formulation or through understanding. Either may lead to an act of innovation.

Creativity. The last aspect, creativity, may also be the beginning of the first aspect, hunger. To transform is to engage in a constant circle or spiral that has neither beginning nor end, which is why the metaphor of the circle or spiral has been used almost universally as a symbol of wholeness. To participate in this process is to engage with life fully in action inherent to humankind. Jung elaborates:

> The richness of the human psyche and its essential character are probably determined by this reflective instinct. Reflection re-enacts the process of excitation and carries the stimulus over into a series of images which, if the impetus is strong enough, are reproduced in some form of expression. This may take place directly, for instance in speech, or may appear in the form of abstract thought, dramatic representation, or ethical conduct; or again, in a scientific achievement or a work of art.[58]

Such series of images form the basis of activity, whatever its shape and form. In this sense, a creative act feeds psychological aspects, and psychological aspects, in turn, feed creative acts. This progression is not linear but circular. One implication is that the capacity for change, either as individuals or as an organization, is not finite. As long as there is energy available for the process, transformation continues. This book demonstrates how the nature of change management, and of change itself, is recursive and can therefore best be served by a methodology that is both flexible and rigorous. Archetypal psychology and mythology provide both, since each is grounded in multiplicity necessary to hold creative potential and to deepen that potential in both individual and organization.

Jung labels his five groups of instinctive factors "ectopsychic" and theorizes that they can be located in the place of story. In other words, these factors can be discovered in narrative expressions. Such a tale is what I refer to as a *corporate mythology*. The interaction between the individual and the organization can generate oppositional force that may lead to the Transcendent Function, the possibility of creating a third *thing*, "A tertium quid," Jung calls it, that transcends both.

The shuttling to and fro of arguments and affects represents the transcendent function of opposites. The confrontation of the two positions generates a tension charged with energy and creates a living, third thing—not a logical still-birth in accordance with the principle *tertium non datur* but a movement out of the suspension between opposites, a living birth that leads to a new level of being, a new situation. The transcendent function manifests itself as a quality of conjoined opposites.[59]

To create this new level of being, this new situation, is the foundation of economic enterprise. Our ability to innovate, to push beyond our current intellectual understanding and formulate something new, defines the creative process. Furthermore, the process of creativity is instinctive to the human race and, whether conscious or not, it is very active and alive in the corporate environment.

To move beyond a theoretical construct is mandatory if any exploration of theory is to have practical ramifications. In a letter to a colleague, Jung cautions:

Theoretical formulations give one absolutely no idea of the practice, which is infinitely more multifaceted and alive than any theory could convey. Nor is it the task of theory to paint a picture of life, but rather to create a workmanlike language which is satisfied with conventional signs.[60]

It is to the workmanlike language of Joseph Campbell that I now turn.

Notes—The MetaMythology of C.G. Jung:

1.   Jung, CW8: 233.

2.   Hillman, Re-Visioning Psychology, 112. This book is my personal favourite of the books written by Hillman to-date.

3.   Hillman, Kinds of Power, 219.

4.   Hillman, The Myth of Analysis, 12.

5.   Jung, Memories, Dreams, Reflections, 302. The biography of C.G. Jung recorded and written by Aniela Jaffé. In the spring of 1957, at the age of 81, Jung undertook the telling of his life story. He continued to work on sections of the manuscript until his death on June 6, 1961. This book explores the complexities of Jung's own thought process and many readers have used this book as an entry to his work.

6.   David Bohm, Quantum Theory, 74. A classic in quantum physics, this book provides a formulation of quantum theory in terms of qualitative and imaginative concepts beyond classical theory. Not for the faint of heart! Bohm was Emeritus Professor of Theoretical Physics at Birkbeck College at the University of London. The reader may wish to start with 'Science, Order and Creativity' written by Bohm and F. David Peat where the authors go beyond a narrow and fragmented view of nature and embrace a more holistic view of the creative process. Another entry to Bohm's work may be found in 'On Creativity' where he explores the relationship between art and science, including his paradigm of nested orders. Bohm's model presents two interpenetrating activities of the mind—imaginative and rational insight and imaginative and rational fancy. He explores the necessity of suspension of judgment in order to create and the process of creativity in its own right.

7.   Hillman, The Myth of Analysis, 8.

8.   Jung, CW8: 248. Of the three modalities described by Jung, this book will primarily address the issue of conscious and unconscious knowledge (commonly called tacit knowledge in OD books) or "the way things are done around here" in plain English. In later writings, an exploration of the third modality, the mind/body connection, will be made.

9.   Jung, CW8: 256.

10. Jung, CW8: 132.

11. Jung, CW8: 158.

12. Jung, CW8: 250. For further exploration of Jung's Psychology of Types or Typology, the work done by Meyers and Briggs is commonly used in organizational settings. The MBTI or Meyers-Briggs Type Indicator is a popular psychological assessment that has proven statistical validity. Refer to "Gifts Differing" by Isabel Briggs Meyers with Peter B. Meyers, which is the classic in understanding personality type. For additional reading, William Bridges is one of my favourites. See "The Character of Organizations" for the use of personality type in organizational development. "Transitions" and "The Way of Transition" for management of change both personal and professional.

13. Jung, CW9ii: 2.

14. Hillman, The Myth of Analysis, 37.

15. Jung, CW8:251.

16. Ibid.

17. Hillman, The Myth of Analysis, 31.

18. Jung, CW16: 454.

19. Jung, CW8: 142.

20. Jung, CW12: 186.

21. Jung, CW11: 391.

22. Jung, CW12: 259.

23. Jung, CW12: 186.

24. Hillman, The Myth of Analysis, 34.

25. Jung, CW8: 131.

26. Jung, CW4: 606.

27. Jung, CW6: 825.

28. Jung, CW12: 28.

29. Bond, Living Myth, 24. Bond's book is an excellent resource for any reader wishing to explore personal myth. Living Myth explores the dilemma of how to live life creatively through the use of mythology. An inviting book to read and I highly recommend it.

30. Jung, Letters 1, 483.

31. Jung, Memories, Dreams, Reflections (or in future, MDR), 340.

32. Jung, CW8: 139.

33. Jung, CW8: 145.

34. Jung, CW8: 173.

35. Ibid, 174.

36. Ibid, 177.

37. Ibid, 177.

38. Jung, CW18: 39.

39. Jung, CW18: 43.

40. Jung, CW18: 72.

41. Jung, Nietzsche's Zarathustra: Notes of the Seminar given in 1934-1939, 795.

42. Jung, CW8: 181.

43. Jung, The Undiscovered Self, 141.

44. Jung, CW16: 432.

45. Jung, Modern Man in Search of a Soul, 217.

46. Jung, CW11: 497.

47. Buckingham and Coffman, First Break All the Rules, 33.

48. Ibid, 34.

49. Ibid, 32.

50. Buckingham and Clifton, Now, Discover Your Strengths, 6.

51. Jung, CW8: 246.

52. Jung, CW8: 236.

53. Ibid.

54. Jung, CW8: 238.

55. Jung, CW8: 240.

56. Jung, CW15: 121.

57. Jung, CW8: 243.

58. Jung, CW8: 242.

59. Jung, CW8: 189.

60. Jung, Letters 1: 324.

Stages: The Heroic Journey

Finding Recognition, Relationship and Meaning in Everyday Life
Leading to Corporate Alignment, Integration and Engagement.

6. Celebration—Creativity

1. Innocence

2. The Call—Hunger

C
O
R
E

5. Breakthrough—Reflection

3. Initiation—Sexuality

4. The Ordeal—Activity

Joseph Campbell
and the Heroic Journey

Joseph Campbell believed that there was a myth that crossed all cultural barriers, all age groups, gender, and race. He called it a monomyth and described this role in *The Hero with a Thousand Faces.*[1] He made his views on mythology and the Hero's Journey popular with the general public in the PBS *Power of Myth* series hosted by Bill Moyers, aired in the late 1980s just before Campbell's death.

Campbell claimed that the story of the hero is as old as time itself; understanding that the story of the hero is one that all individuals follow, for aware or not, the Heroic Path can and does mirror a life. Whether Campbell's body of work is considered scholarly or not is debated; I will make no claim here as to its scholarly value. Campbell termed the Hero's Journey a monomyth, a term he borrowed from author James Joyce in *Finnegans Wake*. My interest in Campbell's work is a practical one, for I have found no other model that provides such easy access by people to the world of mythological systems. Using the Heroic Journey as a life-stage model resonates with every individual in an organizational setting, regardless of their age or race. Whether or not Campbell's concept of a monomyth is accurate, I have yet to find an individual that does not recognize and, more importantly, is able to personally identify and connect with this journey. The Heroic Journey provides a common language easily accessible to all. Campbell offers a more descriptive insight:

> Everywhere, no matter what the sphere of interest (whether religious, political, or personal), the really creative acts are represented as those deriving from some sort of dying to the world; and what happens in the interval of the hero's nonentity, so that he comes back as one reborn, made great and filled with creative power, mankind is also unanimous in declaring. We shall have only to follow, therefore, a multitude of heroic figures through the classic stages of the universal adventure in order to see again what has always been revealed. This will help us to understand not only the meaning of those images for contemporary life, but also the singleness of the human spirit in its aspirations, powers, vicissitudes, and wisdom.[2]

The universal adventure to which Campbell refers provides a map of the territory of the Heroic Journey. As such, it provides an entry into the world of corporate life and, indeed, can be used to parallel the existence of the organization as well as the individual. Many business books have been written that utilize the idea of the Hero/ine, but most play at a superficial level, failing to address the power of the archetype itself.

To use a depth or archetypal psychological approach to organizational culture necessitates deepening our view in order to access the *archai,* or the first principles of the organization. Those first principles come from the individuals who founded or gave birth to the organization. The map of the Heroic Journey can be used as a way of exploring the associations made by individuals that will, in turn, help re-iterate and further clarify and/or identify those foundational beliefs. Such identification of foundational beliefs leads to sustainable branding of any organization and this process will be explored in later works.

In exploring the politics of myth, Robert Ellwood examines the work of Campbell and offers the following insight:

> His message supreme above all was that all myths are really about oneself, one's profoundest identity, the innermost self still waiting to be found and realized. Campbell's conviction was that myths are not past but present, embodying the eternal essence of life.[3]

Recognizing that myth is both current and past allows for one to develop the myth as a vehicle toward the future. Using or employing a mythic approach can help identify what myths or belief systems are being lived by members of an organization. I will begin by addressing the individual and show how Campbell's Heroic Journey can be used in an organizational setting. Campbell argues:

> The hero, therefore, is the man or woman who has been able to battle past his personal and local historical limitations to the generally valid, normally human forms. Such a one's visions, ideas, and inspirations come pristine from the primary spring of human life and thought. Hence they are eloquent, not of the present, disintegrating society and psyche, but of the unquenched source through which society is reborn. The hero has died as a modern man; but as eternal man—perfected, unspecific, universal man—he has been reborn.[4]

In his classes on mythology at Sarah Lawrence, Campbell advised his students to follow their bliss in order to reach that unquenched source. Not in the sense of a drugged-out state or a pollyanna-like feel good group-hug; but in the sense to follow the deepest desire within that drives a life forward into the unknown. No individual lives the life originally planned, for life itself intervenes. Each individual will experience loss of some kind in life and will be forced to come to terms with that loss. To have passion for something or someone denotes previous suffering; the word *passion*, borrowed from Old French and Middle English, means to suffer or endure loss.[5] It is only through such losses that passions become evident, become clear. To "follow your bliss," as directed by Campbell, means to follow lived passion; to heed the knowledge so dearly paid for through suffering and loss. Campbell suggests that the Hero/ine can be one who is either appreciated by society or one who is mocked. In either case, the Hero/ine finds that the symbols or images currently available are not working.

The composite Hero/ine of this monomyth is a personage of exceptional gifts. "Frequently he is honored by his society, frequently unrecognized or disdained. He and/or the world in which he finds himself suffers from a symbolic deficiency."[6]

To "follow your bliss" is a path where an individual speaks his or her truth which ability is a gift in itself. Jung called this authentic voice "individuation," the courage to be one's self. Such an act is sometimes dangerous in an organizational setting if the individual harbors a different belief than a more senior member of the group or the collective group. To claim an authentic voice is to claim leadership, even for an instant. To choose to serve personal belief or core values rather than enhance personal career goals in the face of opposition is to embark on a Hero's Journey. There is no return without consequence, either to career or personal core value system.

The Heroic Adventure

The Heroic Adventure, according to Campbell, can be generalized as follows:

> The mythological hero, setting forth from his commonday hut or castle is lured, carried away, or else voluntarily proceeds, to the threshold of adventure. There he encounters a shadow presence that guards the passage. The hero may defeat or conciliate this power and go alive into the kingdom of the dark (brother-battle, dragon-battle, offering, charm) or be slain by the opponent and descend into death (dismemberment, crucifixion). Beyond the threshold, then, the hero journeys through a world of unfamiliar yet strangely intimate forces, some of which severely threaten him (tests), some of which give magical aid (helpers). When he arrives at the nadir of the mythological round, he undergoes a supreme ordeal and gains his reward. The triumph may be represented as the hero's sexual union with the goddess-mother of the world (sacred marriage), his recognition by the father-creator (father atonement), his own divinization (apotheosis), or again—if the powers have blessed the hero, he now sets forth under their protection (emissary); if not, he flees and is pursued (transformational flight, obstacle

flight). At the return threshold the transcendental powers must remain behind; the hero re-emerges from the kingdom of dread (return, resurrection). The boon that he brings restores the world (elixir).[7]

To "follow your bliss," it is necessary to claim the power to choose to undertake this journey. Such an act involves risk, as the individual becomes vulnerable to loss. The choice might be refused. The choice may be ridiculed. But, if the choice is not made, a deeper loss may be sustained. To live an inauthentic life means never to stand fast in personal beliefs or in a coherent value system and instead choose personal or organizational safety over individuality. Thus the importance of the Heroic Journey, as it provides a visual image for the territory of choice towards individuation and the foundation by which an organization creates a sustainable brand.

This book examines the five of the stages of this model as proposed by Campbell as stages that will be useful in promoting clearer communication in an atmosphere of change, whether it be individual or organizational. Most importantly, these stages provide a visual map or image that can act as a container for tacit knowledge, which, as stated above, are the stories that best represent both the soul of the individual and the soul of the organization on the path to individuation.

Innocence

This is the place of beginnings. A decision has been made to change aspects of a career or to change aspects of the organization. In either case, the traditional way of being is to shift. Such a change may be freely chosen or imposed. It may come as a result of a merger of two organizations where two cultures must combine; it may be a personal promotion or failure, or it may be a change in circumstance in one's personal life, such as marriage or divorce, or an illness or death of someone close to the individual. Campbell turned to the mythologies of past civilizations for guidance to suggest that such aid is available to all who seek it:

> When we turn now [...] to consider the numerous strange rituals that have been reported from the primitive tribes and great civilizations of the past, it becomes apparent that the purpose and actual effort of these was to conduct people across the difficult thresholds of transformation that demand a change in the patterns not only of conscious but also of unconscious life.[8]

Such a demand for change may come from what Campbell termed a "Call." Whether such a call is answered or not, the old way of being is to be forcibly bent to a new circumstance. A brief overview of the five stages of the Journey will be outlined here and then explored in detail in the following chapters.

The Call

To follow this map of the Hero consciously means to view individual circumstance from a mythic perspective. Campbell suggests that a death is required:

> But whether small or great, and nó matter what the stage or grade of life, the call rings us the curtain, always, on a mystery of transfiguration—a rite, or moment, of spiritual passage, which, when complete, amounts to a dying and a birth. The familiar life horizon has been outgrown; the old concepts, ideals, and emotional patterns no longer fit; the time for the passing of a threshold is at hand.[9]

There is no guarantee that a "call" is a pleasant situation; indeed, most "calls" result from a perceived or actual loss. As the call "rings us the curtain," it serves as the beginning of the transformational journey. Depending on the circumstances in one's life, this call may occur not just once but many times. Death and rebirth may become a repetitive theme. The world as a result of this circumstance has changed and a demand placed on the individual to change with it. The individual must claim his or her own story as well as the right to live it. To seek others who share commitment and common beliefs provides a group of allies for the new and unknown journey. In a corporation, such a shared story can be considered the rock-solid foundation of the organization and the essence of its corporate brand. To lose this living link to the story is to lose the ability to choose, or in sequence, to change. A spiritual journey is called for; beliefs will be tested and fear will surface to deflect one from the journey. The Call formulates the beginning of the Core, the essence of the individual.

> The first stage of the mythological journey—which we have designated the "call to adventure"—signifies that destiny has summoned the hero and transferred his spiritual center of gravity from within the pale of his society to a zone unknown.[10]

Not everyone willingly participates, and some will refuse to answer, for the unknown represents too great a leap of faith.

In *Pathways to Bliss*, Campbell revisits his work on the Heroic Journey and states:

> If the call is heeded, however, the individual is invoked to engage in a dangerous adventure. It's always a dangerous adventure because you're moving out of the known sphere altogether into the great beyond. I call this crossing the threshold. This is the crossing from the conscious into the unconscious world, but the

unconscious world is represented in many, many, many different images, depending on the culture mythos.[11]

Crossing the threshold can be considered a rite of passage, or initiation.

Initiation

Initiation is meant to be painful, for it marks the ending of one state of being and the beginning of a new. In ancient times, it involved bloodletting of some kind, a ritual that demanded courage. Initiation marks the place of those who are brave and those who are cowards. To claim or to choose passion requires an act of bravery. There will be those who can't muster the requisite courage, and thus fall into the misery of possessing a job they have no love for, or a profession they pretend to serve. The Hero/ine must make the courageous step forward and claim the Call to Adventure for its effect on the individual both personally and professionally. In *Pathways to Bliss*, Campbell expands on the use of one of his favourite metaphors to describe this place of being caught between a rock and a hard place or, "clashing rocks" and explains:

> We live, on this side of the mystery, in the realm of the pairs of opposites: true and false, light and dark, good and evil, male and female, and all that dualistic rational worldview. One can have an intuition that is beyond good and evil, that goes beyond pairs of opposites—that's the opening of this gateway into the mystery. But it's just one of those little intuitive flashes, because the conscious mind comes back again and closes the door. The idea in the hero adventure is to walk bodily through the door into the world where the dualistic rules don't apply.[12]

Walking through this "door" leads the Hero/ine deeper into the journey, the Ordeal. It is here that your faith and courage will be tested.

The Ordeal

Campbell continues his deepening of the metaphor:

> This motif is known also, mythologically, as the active door. This mythic device appears in American Indian stories, in Greek stories, in Eskimo stories, in stories from all over. It is an archetypal image that communicates the sense of going past judgment.[13]

Those who love the status quo will attack the Hero/ine viciously. In a perusal through history, one sees that those who have held to innovative ideas have been sorely tested. To survive this test of loyalty to one's own choice presents difficult tests. The Hero/ine may falter under the attack. Now is the time to look around and discover who is also undergoing this trial. If allies can be found that hold a shared value system, the Hero/ine will survive the Ordeal and be stronger for the initiation. Campbell ventures to say:

> Once you have crossed the threshold, if it really is your adventure—if it is a journey that is appropriate to your deep spiritual need or readiness—helpers will come along the way to provide magical aid. [...] The deeper you get into this gauntlet, the heavier the resistance. You are coming into areas of the unconscious that have been repressed: the shadow, the anima/animus, and the rest of the unintegrated self; it is that repression system that you have to pass through. This, of course, is where the magical aid is most required. [14]

If there are no obvious allies, perhaps the Hero/ine is with the wrong tribe. If no allies are apparent, perhaps the ally that you are seeking is within. Campbell terms this condition apotheosis, where you realize that *you* are what you are seeking. [15]

In organizational terms, the common core value system can be explored to ensure that there is a common understanding of language. Incongruence will produce gaps in communication where an organization says one thing and does another. If the core value system is truly shared and repeatedly communicated, the organization has cohesion and a workable living brand.

Breakthrough

Once the Hero/ine has found a tribe that shares this level of commitment, then innovation and growth become normative. There is no need to attack another because now a sense of self has been achieved that allows for both the individual journey and a collective vision.

In organizational terms, there is no "buy-in," for there is nothing to sell. Instead, what arises is a sense of community that has a unified purpose. Goals may change as circumstances alter but there is no major discomfort or distress. The foundation of the community rests in its shared beliefs, which constitute its core value system. In this case, the Hero/ine can fight many battles because the safety and stability of the community allows for separation and return. The community supports the individual journey as it recognizes the value of separation from the status quo seeks an act of innovation that can be returned to the community as the prize or boon. Such a separation necessitates personal growth. In Campbell's words,

The agony of breaking through personal limitations is the agony of spiritual growth. Art, literature, myth and cult, philosophy, and ascetic disciplines are instruments to help the individual past his limiting horizons into spheres of ever-expanding realization.[16]

This expansive realization, Jim Collins in *Good to Great,* calls this Level 5 Leadership.[17] A Level 5 Leader is one who is not an egomaniac. A Level 5 Leader does not create a firm that will fall apart if that leader leaves it. A Level 5 Leader is a Hero/ine that lives his or her values-in-action and serves the organization to which the leader belongs. When an environment is created that permits the growth of such a leader, a community of shared practice is created with a shared, living story that is grounded in a coherent core set of values. Such a process is indeed difficult and many who attempt it fail. But when success does result in this journey, the reward is increased potential. Campbell explains:

> The whole idea is that you've got to bring out again that which you went to recover, the unrealized, unutilized potential in yourself. The whole point of this journey is the reintroduction of this potential into the world; that is to say, to you living in the world. You are to bring this treasure of understanding back and integrate it in a rational life. It goes without saying that this is difficult. Bringing the boon back can be even more difficult than going down into your own depths in the first place.[18]

Celebration

Celebration is an important part of both individual and organizational life. To recognize the Heroes and Heroines within any organization, to give appreciations for the risks taken and the courage exhibited, again helps cement the core foundation on which the organization rests. To tell the stories of each and every Hero/ine allows to form a living history from which to learn. Mentoring becomes a natural event—for those who are drawn to a particular story can gain insight as well as practical, workable tools in how to proceed on their own journey of exploration. To provide concrete guidance may be impossible, for each individual brings a unique skill set. Campbell elaborates:

> How render back into light-world language the speech-defying pronouncements of the dark? How represent on a two-dimensional surface a three-dimensional form, or in a three-dimensional image a multi-dimensional meaning? How translate into terms of "yes" and "no" revelations that shatter into meaninglessness every attempt to define the pairs of opposites? How communicate to

people who insist on the exclusive evidence of their senses the message of the all-generating void?[19]

Those who have the courage to make this story a conscious one in any organization will reap great rewards. To focus only on bottom line profitability sucks the life-blood out of an organization. To demand instant "return on investment" or ROI is to lose sight of the fact that business is about building relationships, and relationships take time. To honor the relationship between the old warrior and the new is to honor the story as a living, breathing entity. When individuals collaborate to compete, a space is created for both/and rather than either/or. To honor the relationship enables both client and employee retention, because the story is one that continues as a living entity. At heart, we are all storytellers and who would not want to be part of a great story?

The value of the Heroic Journey is that it provides a guide that enables a shift in perspective. In order to claim the future, one must also retrieve and re-claim the past. Holding this tension of opposites, two seemingly opposing stances, requires a mental shift that can be made and then expanded through the understanding that archetypal psychology promotes. To use story as a container or *temenos* for this movement or shift in traditional thinking provides a place of comfort. On the future value of the Heroic Journey, perhaps Campbell should have the last word:

> What I think is that a good life is one hero journey after another. Over and over again, you are called to the realm of adventure, you are called to new horizons. Each time, there is the same problem: do I dare? And then if you do dare, the dangers are there, and the help also, and the fulfillment or the fiasco. There's always the possibility of a fiasco. But there's also the possibility of bliss.[20]

Notes—Joseph Campbell and the Heroic Journey:

1. Joseph Campbell, The Hero with a Thousand Faces, 36.

2. Ibid.

3. Robert Ellwood, The Politics of Myth, 129. Ellwood's book is an interesting comparison between several scholars of myth. He compares and contrasts various aspects of mythology in terms of practical use.

4. Campbell, The Hero with a Thousand Faces, 20.

5. Barnhart, 544.

6. Campbell, The Hero with a Thousand Faces, 37.

7. Ibid, 245.

8. Ibid, 10.

9. Ibid, 51.

10. Ibid, 58.

11. Campbell, Pathways to Bliss, 114.

12. Ibid.

13. Ibid, 115.

14. Ibid, 116.

15. Ibid, 118.

16. Campbell, The Hero With a Thousand Faces, 190.

17. Jim Collins, Good to Great, 17. This book is one of my personal favourites. Collins compares and contrasts those companies that are good to those that are great. A values-based or archetypal approach is used for personal development that expands into organizational success. Well-written and easy to read.

18. Campbell, Pathways to Bliss, 119.

19. Campbell, The Hero With a Thousand Faces, 218.

20. Campbell, Pathways to Bliss, 133.

Mythopoesis:
Branding from the Inside Out

The study of the belief systems or mythologies inherent in an organization can help illuminate the challenges presented in attempting to change the corporate culture and to create a sustainable corporate brand. The Heroic model as devised by Campbell can enable individual change by means of its visual representation as a tool for finding meaning in images of contemporary life. By combining these two aspects, a working method can be devised that illustrates how systems of belief can be visually represented and then consciously examined. Such examination will increase awareness and allow the individual to participate actively in conscious myth-making, or mythopoesis. Every corporate culture consists of groups of individuals, and each individual has a particular motivation in joining with a particular group or organization. Every individual also brings his or her story into the organization, a collection of life experiences that informs his or her behavior within an organizational context. The collection of individual stories will also be influenced by the stories of the organization itself. Both will inform and potentially transform the other.

The Heroic Journey as a model allows an archetypal exploration into the field of corporate culture and an exploration of future archetypal branding. This approach does not make any claim on validity but instead opens up a field of inquiry. Jung stresses the importance of a framework in dealing with the unconscious; he offers, "a model does not assert that something is *so*, it simply illustrates a particular mode of observation."[1] As any exploration of the unconscious is at best an approximation, a visual map may be of service.

Both individual and organizational story is context-dependent, meaning that the story is constantly changing due to external and internal shifts in perspective or in circumstance. Thus, the use of archetypal psychology as a lens by which to view this living story of individual or of organization has a unique value, as archetypal psychology concerns itself with pluralities of meaning.

According to Jung, our concern with ascribed meaning is an ancient one. Jung asks:

From what source, in the last analysis, do we derive meaning? The forms we use for assigning meaning are historical categories that reach back into the mists of time—a fact we do not take sufficiently into account. Interpretations make use of certain linguistic matrices that are themselves derived from primordial images.[2]

Jung further explains that interpretations or ideas always have some form of historical antecedent such that an awareness of these archetypes can inform and educate through perceived experience.[3] Experience of these ancient forms can be "active personalities in dreams and fantasies" or through another class of archetypes "which one could call the archetypes of transformation." Jung elaborates:

They are not personalities, but are typical situations, places, ways and means, that symbolize the kind of transformation in question. Like the personalities, these archetypes are true and genuine symbols that cannot be exhaustively interpreted, either as signs or allegories.[4]

In accessing and using story in either an individual or organizational context, the story will contain a potential archetype of transformation. By identifying these archetypes through a tool such as the Heroic Journey, a structure may be formed that enables mythopoesis, an act of the imagination in which a prevailing mythic images is reshaped, reformed, and given new life. Behind the concrete particulars of any situation, a mythical move provides a "seeing-through" to the mystery or unconscious beyond, to a field of potential that has not yet been accessed, which cannot be known directly but is rather intuited. Understanding a corporate culture can be thought of as breaking a code. Understanding the why of change is crucial for business because it predicts what people will do, whether employee or client. Archetypes and their associated images provide a form of cultural logic by which to translate either individual or organizational behaviour. By identification of these archetypes of transformation in any given story, a safe space for the story to unfold is created.

Interplay between Instinct and Archetype

Such space can be visualized as an interplay between the individual unconscious and the collective unconscious and their reciprocal inflection. A visual representation of this interplay may assist in explanation. Picture a color spectrum with instinct on one end and archetypal energy on the other, as shown below.

Interplay between Individual and Collective Unconscious

Instinct	Archetype
(red end)	(violet end)

Jung viewed this perpetual interaction as a paradox, since "conscious and unconscious have no clear demarcations, the one beginning where the other leaves off."[5] He observes:

> Archetype and instinct are the most polar opposites imaginable, as can easily be seen when one compares a man who is ruled by his instinctual drives with a man who is seized by the spirit. But, just as between all opposites there obtains so close a bond that no position can be established or even thought of without its corresponding negation, so in this case also "les extremes se touchent." They belong together as correspondences, which is not to say that the one is derivable from the other, but that they subsist side by side as reflections in our own minds of the opposition that underlies all psychic energy. Man finds himself simultaneously driven to act and free to reflect.[6]

Jung's theory suggests that psychic processes behave like a scale along which consciousness "slides."[7] This is one of the reasons I find story so important. The story acts as a container for this psychic slide and contains both the action and the reflection on the action. By careful listening to the story itself, one can locate where psychic energy predominates, flows, or has become fixed. When you find the energy or essence, you find the brand.

The movement between the opposites can become mythopoetic; in other words, the movement becomes the act of assigning meaning to what is experienced, the essence of branding. In this movement of assigning meaning, archetypal psychology is based in phenomenology thus becomes a circular process of knowing through what is experienced. What is experienced becomes memory which acts analogically to further experience. The collection of experiences informs the belief system of the individual. The movement along this spectrum, as Jung understood it, provides the components necessary for the individuation process, the coming of increased consciousness. He elaborates:

> Over against the polymorphism of the primitive's instinctual nature there stands the regulating principle of individuation. Multiplicity and inner division are opposed by an integrative unity whose power is as great as that of the instincts. Together they form a pair of opposites necessary for self-regulation,

often spoken of as nature and spirit. These conceptions are rooted in psychic conditions between which human consciousness fluctuates like the pointer on the scales.[8]

To address and, more importantly, to understand this regulating principle of individuation challenges one's capacity to enter such a mysterious terrain. Because of this struggle, the Heroic Journey paradigm as a developmental tool may be implemented to describe either individual or organizational story by serving as a container for this process of raising the level of consciousness awareness.

Jung believed that for a culture to advance, the process must begin with the individual. For an organization to make a cultural shift, again the process will begin with the individual as it moves away from the cultural norm. Jung believes that "wherever the cultural process is moving forward, whether in single individuals or in groups, we find a shaking off of collective beliefs."[9] To make a move away from the industrial age toward the knowledge or information age, collective beliefs must be questioned, if not discarded. Jung was adamant regarding the importance of the individual:

> All big organizations that pursue exclusively materialistic aims are the pacemakers of mass-mindedness. The sole possibility of stopping this is the development of consciousness in the single individual, who thereby is rendered immune to the lure of collective organizations. This alone keeps his soul alive, for its life depends on the human relationship. The accent must fall on conscious personalization and not on State organization.[10]

And yet, those collective organizational beliefs can also be carried within the container of story and used to further the relationship between individuals. Stories told in an organizational setting carry the core values and beliefs of the organization in the same way that the stories told by an individual carry personal beliefs, prejudices and core values. All provide information that can be utilized in understanding behavior. By having a common model such as the Heroic Journey so easily accessible by any individual in the organization, similarities and differences can be explored in a visual context. It has been my experience as an organizational consultant that such a visual context allows each story to be honored and expressed in such a way that is more easily understood by both self and others. Employing this type of developmental tool may enable a more effective form of communication in an organizational context and promotes both generational and cultural diversity.

I cannot emphasize enough the immediate transformative effect when image is used as a developmental tool in an organizational setting. To capture such an internal image, I use a variety of postcards or photographs that can be utilized to provoke or stimulate imaginative projection.

The images evoke different meanings for each individual and therein lies the value. The plurality of meaning expressed by values inherent in any group becomes immediately apparent. As such, the image becomes a vehicle for communication in that it provides a starting point whereby each individual claims a personal interpretation as to how that image relates to the current situation or context. To claim a personal interpretation is to claim responsibility for the self, to be willing to step away from collective beliefs and stand firm on potentially new ground. Jung believed that most individuals walk in "shoes too small."[11] To step into larger shoes is a necessary ingredient to advance consciousness. Jung concludes:

> Therefore an advance always begins with individuation, that is to say with the individual, conscious of his isolation, cutting a new path through hitherto untrodden territory. To do this he must first return to the fundamental facts of his own being, irrespective of all authority and tradition, and allow himself to become conscious of his distinctiveness. If he succeeds in giving collective validity to his widened consciousness, he creates a tension of the opposites that provides the stimulation which culture needs for its further progress.[12]

In organizational terms, such an advance in consciousness unlocks the door to innovation and provides a key to future growth and a successful brand. In individual terms, such widened consciousness produces a core value system.

Expanding Instinct as Image and Archetype as Thought

In terms of Jung's model of a psychic slide, two post-Jungian theorists will further elaborate this tension of the opposites; the two polarities, instinct and archetype; and how each polarity may be utilized to further increase consciousness. Further, to view also Collins and Porras' model (shown in italics below) that incorporates both a core ideology and a drive for progress through this aperture of polarity, an application of Jungian theory will provide further clarity. The model from *Built to Last* describes a corporation but also carried similarities with the process of individuation, indicating the potential movement or "slide" between the two polarities. Such movement creates a psychic space for the transcendent function to become operational.

Polarity Slide between Core Ideology (or Artistic Formulation) and Drive for Progress (or Meaning)

Instinct	Archetype
(red end)	(violet end)
Image	Thought
Artistic Formulation	Meaning

Core Ideology: (Or Artistic Formulation)	Drive for Progress: (Or Meaning)
Provides continuity and stability. In providing a metaphor by which to describe and/or experience archetypal energy, the metaphor or image allows continuity of interpretation for the individual.	*Urges continual change.* An archetype has no form, simply energy. Thus form can be constantly changing.
Plants a relatively fixed stake in the ground. An archetypal image can provide a place to begin, a starting point by which to move forward. The archetypal image gives a container, a *temenos* for archetypal energy.	*Impels constant movement.* An archetype has no fixed state, it thus can be constantly moving or shifting.
Limits possibilities and directions for the company. Provides a container in which to work, allows for a fixed starting point by which the individual can begin the process of individuation.	*Expands the number and variety of possibilities that the company can consider.* Polytheistic—multiple meanings are available.
Has clear content. Expressed by or held by image or metaphor.	*Can be content-free.* Expressed by multiplicity, multiple interpretations and expressions.

Core Ideology: (Or Artistic Formulation)	Drive for Progress: (Or Meaning)
Installing a core ideology is, by its very nature, a conservative act.	*Expressing the drive for progress can lead to dramatic, radical and revolutionary change.*
Provides a solid ground, which can provide a breakthrough in thinking which can be expressed or expanded in multiple possibilities.	Allows for a breakthrough in thinking which can be captured by image or metaphor.
Permits the individual to establish the core ideology of the Self.	After establishing core ideology of the Self, the individual can expand conscious awareness by starting this process anew.

James Hillman: Image as Instinct

For Jungian Analyst James Hillman, psyche is image. He urges that the individual stay with the image and not be distracted by the ego's demand for comprehension: "We sin against the imagination whenever we ask an image for its meaning, requiring that images be translated into concepts."[13] For Hillman, it is mandatory to "see through" the image, to stay with the particulars of a personal viewpoint or code of experience rather than focus on the literal object to ask what is this "like," not what does this "mean." Hillman suggests that such a stance will broaden awareness or consciousness, by incorporating as many different views as possible before any interpretation is attempted.

Jung ventured to say that without consciousness there would, practically speaking, be no world, for the world exists for us only insofar as it is consciously reflected by a psyche and suggests that "consciousness is a precondition of being."[14]

In order for a current state of consciousness to be expanded, Hillman argues that interpretations must remain flexible, if indeed such interpretations are even attempted. To attempt interpretations, caution must be exercised so that the interpretation does not become fixed or literal. To reside in the image and not fixate on the literal object invites a plurality of meaning to find expression and does not limit the image to only one motif. In allowing for such plurality of meaning, in speaking of his work on the transcendent function, Jung states:

> Where the principle of creative formulation predominates, the material is continually varied and increased until a kind of condensation of motifs into more or less stereotyped symbols takes place. These stimulate the creative fantasy

and serve chiefly as aesthetic motifs. This tendency leads to the aesthetic problem of artistic formulation. [15]

Hillman's body of work represents artistic formulation as defined by Jung. Hillman has based his work primarily on a sensate mode of representation, emphasizing the aesthetics of any given situation rather than a reductionistic interpretive mode. He has demanded that the field of psychology view its own shadow; that pathologizing can lead into a deeper sickness. He urges staying with the image; those images are what are seen *through*. The image can be construed as a *temenos*—the container that logic works through to provide additional images that will lead to additional meaning. Hillman sees image as the "and" or "both"—referring to conscious and unconscious contents that logic works in order to comprehend the world; he demands that we return to "soul-making" to allow the soul a free form of expression without labeling such expression as pathology. If soul-making is in the hands of the individual as an imaginal activity, then it is possible to view either an individual or an organizational system from the archetypal model of the Heroic Journey.

Such a visual representation will allow a "seeing-through," as prescribed by Hillman, that does not claim any particular view as pathological. Campbell's visual map of the Heroic Journey becomes a *temenos* by which individual and organizational stories can be viewed without pathological interpretation.

Hillman's body of work leans towards the red end or instinctual aspect of the spectrum as envisioned by Jung and as cited above. As Hillman stays within the phenomenon itself, the actual experience, he translates the experience into image or aesthetic motifs. Staying with the image encourages intensification and avoids concrete depiction. He elaborates on image and states: "there shall be no definition, which limits and cuts, but rather amplification, which extends and connects."[16] In *Healing Fiction*, Hillman continues to amplify his own interpretation:

> Images are effects of their co-relative causes, and they have effects because of these causes. Co-relation implies simultaneity, cause and effect are both present together at the same moment: the archetype is *in* the image.[17]

Campbell's visual representation of the Heroic Journey is archetypal and encourages the making of the map while not specifically delimiting each stage of the journey. Instead, he also amplifies the process, extending and connecting aspects of the journey to the individuation process. This instinctual end of the spectrum could be considered the modality of the physical body, or soma. Jung includes in this modality as "patterns of behaviour":

> In view of the structure of the body, it would be astonishing if the psyche were the only biological phenomenon not to show clear traces of its evolutionary history, and it is altogether probable that these marks are closely connected with the instinctual base. Instinct and the archaic mode meet in the biological conception of the "pattern of behaviour." There are, in fact, no amorphous instincts, as every instinct bears in itself the pattern of its situation. Always it fulfils an image, and the image has fixed qualities. [...] The same is true also of man; he has in him these *a priori* instinct-types which provide the occasion and the pattern for his activities, in so far as he functions instinctively. [...] We may say that the image represents the *meaning* of the instinct. [18]

To turn now to the exploration of meaning, the other end of the spectrum represents the unconscious. Jung believed this arena to be pure undifferentiated archetypal energy. Physics is also the study of energy and both Jung, as a psychologist, and as physicist attempts to describe how that energy may manifest. Physicists study the outside observable world; Jung studied both the interior and exterior of the psyche, its dynamics, its potential, and its creativity. The idea of a creative world-principle is a projected perception of the living essence in man himself. Jung believed that "in order to avoid all vitalistic misunderstandings, one would do well to regard this essence in the abstract, as simply *energy.*"[19]

From Jung's perspective, this energy can take two forms; actual and potential:

> The distinction between force and energy is a conceptual necessity, for energy is really a concept and, as such, does not exist objectively in the phenomena themselves but only in the specific data of experience. In other words, energy is always experienced specifically as motion and force when actual, and a state or condition when potential. Psychic energy appears when actual, in the specific, dynamic phenomena of the psyche, such as instinct, wishing, willing, affect, attention, capacity for work, etc. which make up the psychic forces. When potential, energy shows itself in specific achievements, possibilities, aptitudes, attitudes, etc. which are its various states.[20]

The basis of Jung's metamythology incorporates these polarities: actual and potential are two separate states that produce an immense tension within the individual. If that tension can be held, a third thing may arise, Jung's tertum quid, which Jung called the transcendent function—that mystery which holds the answer to the tension and a resultant expansion of our consciousness.

As stated previously, Jung asserted that the psychological "transcendent function" arises from the union of conscious and unconscious contents.[21] It is a balance point between actual and potential.

To use quantum theory as an analogy may be helpful. Quantum theory states that there exists energy that is contained in a both/and place, a place of potential, where duality does not exist. As such, it may provide a reconciliation point between the integration of Psyche and Soma, mind and matter. Jung suspected that the work for our time would be in such an area of integration, before further understanding of the Psyche would be possible.

Using Jung's modality of Psyche/Soma as the bridge, suggests that integration is possible. The split between spirit and matter can be accessed by a common ground: archetypal psychology. As Jung suggests:

> [...] from the existence of these two categories ethical, aesthetic, intellectual, social, and religious systems of value arise which in the end determine how the dynamic factors in the psyche are to be used. Perhaps it would not be too much to say that the most crucial problems of the individual and of society turn upon the way the psyche functions in regard to spirit and matter.[22]

Quantum theory reveals that the *intent* of the observer *creates* the form taken by the energy. As such, the act of self-reflection becomes part of this psychic equation to bring an additional option for observation of these systems of value. Such observation becomes an act of imaginal play. According to Hillman:

> The ground of being in the depths is not just my own personal ground; it is the universal support of each, to which each finds access through an inner connection. We meet one another as well through reflecting the collective unconscious as we do through expressing ourselves in personal communications. Healing takes place in the same way, depending not so much upon my effect on you or your effect on me, but upon the effect of critical moments, archetypal events, welling up from within and reflected in our meeting.[23]

The act of reflection may be construed as a critical moment, a necessary component of imaginal play that allows for a collaboration of conscious and unconscious content.

Wolfgang Geigerich: Archetype as Thought

Such reflection has been taken up by Jungian Analyst Wolfgang Geigerich, who presents an alternative path toward integration of Psyche and Matter through logical formulation. Geigerich qualifies the use of image; instead he advocates a return to abstract thought. He could be considered on the opposite end of Jung's psychic slide:

> Where, on the other hand, the principle of understanding predominates, the aesthetic aspect is of relatively little interest and may occasionally even be felt as a hindrance. Instead, there is an intensive struggle to understand the *meaning* of the unconscious product.[24]

Geigerich will not limit the soul to image. He argues in *The Soul's Logical Life*, "To be sure, Jung said '*Bild ist Seele*' ('Image is soul'). But image is soul because image is thought *represented* in pictorial form."[25] The danger is the reduction to a purely pictorial form in which the form presented may be mistaken as primary, in itself. Geigerich states "[p]sychology would be what holds the opposites apart, and at the same time unites them by exposing itself to their tension and by existing *as* this tension."[26]

Jung felt that one tendency seems to be the regulating principle of the other; both are bound together in a compensatory relationship.[27] Both are needed to ensure a transcendence from the conflict of opposites.

In order to find an integration point in a compensatory relationship, Hillman may be viewed as actual and Geigerich as potential. Quantum theory demands that an energy field be reconstructed as both/and not either/or. The intent of the observer creates the form taken by the energy. It is difficult to hold two opposing views at the same time. There must be an understanding that emphasis must bear on the whole *and* the part. Thus there will always be two states—one potential and one actual. Viewed from this perspective, Jung's concept of individuation takes on additional meaning. If there were an innate drive towards wholeness, towards a unified system of reality, then it would follow that the unconscious aim of the psyche would be to return to the realm of quantum reality. The only method the psyche has for communicating that need is through unconscious processes breaking through into consciousness. As consciousness expands, then access to further potential is increased, and may indeed be unlimited.

Geigerich posits that the form by which the psyche communicates this potential is thinking, "*Geist*," not image. In other words, pure undifferentiated potential that has not yet split into the Psyche/Soma duality. He argues:

Being logical this movement does not occur as a succession in time (now this, now the other). It occurs as the internal logic of one and the same (truly psychological) speaking. What it speaks about cannot be perceived with the senses, it cannot be imagined, it can only be apperceived as thought.[28]

Geigerich maintains that the "image" is reductionistic; by its very nature it contains a context. He agrees that Jung did say, "soul is image" but did not state that "image is soul." Thus Geigerich attempts to remain within an undifferentiated (quantum) state:

As long as one feels that matter and spirit, humans and the cosmos, the opposites of the gender issue, and so on are the real concern of psychology, the soul is still "beside itself," or better *outside* itself, in exile. It is still immersed *and lost* in a concretistic "out there" that it can *observe or envision* and thereby hold away from itself as an "object" *given* to it as the experiencing subject. It can still avoid having to *think*, that is to say, having to realize what it is delaying with is its very own (its own thoughts) from the outset.[29]

However, if such is the case, then Hillman's and Geigerich's perspectives are required to comprehend this movement on a psychic slide. They are two sides of the same coin. Both Hillman and Geigerich force the question of how to see the relationship between theory and reality, potential and actual. Reducing image to a pictorial representation would be equivalent to reducing logic or "Geist" to mathematical symbolism. Each contains the other and cannot therefore be reduced to a simplistic form without loss of the referent to what cannot be named, but only inferred. The possibilities of the interrelation of this information exchange become clear. Jung agrees and states:

As far as it is possible at this stage to draw more general conclusions, we could say that aesthetic formulation needs understanding of the meaning, and understanding needs aesthetic formulation. The two supplement each other to form the transcendent function.[30]

Holding the Tension of the Opposites:
The Transcendent Function

The transcendent function is an appropriate and effective analogy for the differences in focus between Jungian analysts such as Hillman and Geigerich because it provides a ready tool for integration. Perhaps the work of Geigerich is less generally accessible as he remains in the quantum realm of abstraction, but he does speak to the difficulty of holding two opposing modes of thought:

> Psychology has to establish itself in the uroboros, as the unity of the identity and difference of the opposites. But because the uroboros contains both identity and difference, our myth must not be one-sidedly seen as the description of one archetypal instance either. It is also the unity of a linear sequence of events *and* a dialectical simultaneity, the unity of medium and message.[31]

Jung maintained that "energy in itself is neither good nor bad, neither useful nor harmful, but neutral, since everything depends on the *form* into which energy passes. Form gives energy its quality."[32] Hillman and Geigerich offer varying forms in which they place their understanding of this energy called Psyche. To hold the place of "both" is certainly difficult. Geigerich asks that the reader understand:

> it is the entire dialectic of imagining (personifying, objectifying, reifying, ontologizing) *and* de-imagining (sublation, dissolution, putrefaction into logical movement). The Notion or Truth is the unity of its fulfillment *and* the various stages of approaching it.[33]

Hillman also speaks to a sense of unity:

> "[T]he soul's wants are the ground of psychic purposefulness. The soul seeks the initiatory mystery (*teletè*) which also means fulfillment. The soul's wants are teleological because it is not differentiated, not complete, and not conjoined, the individuation process whose goal (*telos*) is wholeness answers the soul's wants.[34]

Quantum theory states that the wave/particle split is but a pool of information established by exchange and dialogue between the wave/particle and the observer. Information simply means to "put form-in"—to "in-form." Could it be that the psyche is but a pool of information that may manifest in an image? That pure abstraction is hard to hold without forming a representation, whether it is as symbol, mathematical notation or imaginal form? This aspect of wholeness in quantum theory is referred to as "phase entanglement." A part cannot be separated from the whole without affecting both. Jung elaborates:

> Moreover, the instincts are not vague and indefinite by nature, but are specifically formed motive forces which, long before there is any consciousness, and

in spite of any degree of consciousness later on, pursue their inherent goals. Consequently they form very close analogies to the archetypes, so close, in fact, that there is good reason for supposing that the archetypes are the unconscious images of the instincts themselves, in other words, that they are patterns of instinctual behavior. [35]

Individual perspective will determine either the position, the actual as formulated by Hillman, or movement, the abstract potential as formulated by Geigerich. Hillman remains in the sensate realm of the body, Soma, and his focus is mainly form. Geigerich remains in the world of the mind, Psyche, and his focus is mainly content. An individual cannot see pure thought but can see its effect through a manifested form or image. Returning to this analogy of quantum theory, particle and wave cannot be differentiated unless by the intent of an observer. Geigerich's concerns rest in the potentialities whereas Hillman's concerns rest in the manifestation of such abstractions. Therefore, both theorists remain in compensatory relationship in the act of creation. Such compensatory work is through the modality of mind and spirit—uniting Psyche and Soma and fulfilling the fifth psychic drive as postulated by Jung: creativity.

I understand an individual mind as a quantum field, one in which potential is activated by intent. Definitions of theory and praxis must be complementary. If Hillman and Geigerich appear to clash in their basic assumptions and if each provides an explanation of experience, even if partial, it is reasonable nonetheless to assume that both theorists engage a larger view which remains to be formulated. Both point to the concept of a unity, albeit in different forms. Both struggle with language that only approximates such a unified theory.

Perhaps this is the task of the Post-Jungians, Jungian theorists after Jung—and also of physicists—to find a way of describing such abstraction in terms that do not reduce the unified whole to a mere part. Such theorists are to continue the dialogue in theory and praxis until a sublated form is created—a complete theory. As Stephen Hawking observes,

> If we do discover a complete theory, it should in time be understandable in broad principle by everyone, not just a few scientists. Then we shall all, philosophers, scientists and just ordinary people, be able to take part in the discussion of the question of why it is that we and the universe exist. If we find the answer to that, it would be the ultimate triumph of human reason—for then we would know the mind of God. [36]

To attempt such a spiritual discovery requires tools. The value of the Heroic Journey is that it is an easily accessible tool that permits, even encourages, the use of image and thought. Philosophers and scientists have been arguing these questions for centuries. Joseph Campbell and his body of work have allowed ordinary people access to this discussion. The map of the Heroic Journey provides a visual starting point for any and all heroes to participate in this dialogue. In the following chapters, I will explore in detail the five stages of the Heroic Journey through this overlay of archetypal psychology and show how the use of the Heroic Journey combined with the metamythology as formulated by C. G. Jung can be understood as two variations on the same insight, both of which provide additional knowledge into an age-old problem.

Heroic Journey as a Mythopoetic Tool in the Interplay between Instinct and Archetype

The decision of whether such attempt could be considered a move towards a complete theory will reside in future research. I am content to offer the Heroic Journey as a mythopoetic tool in order to navigate between the tension of the opposites and, potentially, to provide an archetypal move toward integration between Psyche and Matter. In the research conducted by Collins and Porras, being able to hold this tension of the opposites, the paradox of core ideology and the drive to change is necessary for a visionary company that endures over time. Similarly, it is necessary for an individual to first establish a core ideology, a recognition of the Self, in order to embark on a journey of change. It has been my experience that the powerful metaphor of the Heroic Journey, in conjunction with the psychic drive theory as delineated by Jung, provides the impetus to individuate. Jung issues a challenge:

> The spirit of evil is fear, negation, the adversary who opposes life in its struggle for eternal duration and thwarts every great deed, who infuses into the body the poison of weakness and ago through the treacherous bite of the serpent; he is the spirit of regression, who threatens us with bondage to the mother and with dissolution and extinction in the unconscious. For the hero, fear is a challenge and a task, because only boldness can deliver from fear. And if the risk is not taken, the meaning of life is somehow violated, and the whole future is condemned to hopeless staleness, to a drab grey lit only by will-o'-the-wisps. [37]

The following chapters will amplify each stage of the Heroic Journey, the theory supporting each stage, and provide actual examples of individual courage that resulted in both personal and organizational transformation. My opus has begun.

Notes—The Need for Mythopoesis:

1. Jung, CW8: 381.

2. Jung, CW9i: 67.

3. Jung, CW9i: 69.

4. Jung, CW9i: 80.

5. Jung, CW8: 397.

6. Jung, CW8: 406.

7. Jung, CW8: 408.

8. Jung, CW8: 96.

9. Jung, CW8: 111.

10. Jung, Letters 1: 472.

11. Jung, CW8: 739.

12. Jung, CW8: 111.

13. Hillman, Re-Visioning Psychology, 38.

14. Jung, The Undiscovered Self, 27.

15. Jung, CW8: 173.

16. Hillman, The Myth of Analysis, 31.

17. Hillman, Healing Fiction, 72.

18. Jung, CW8: 398.

19. Jung, CW6: 337.

20. Jung, CW8: 26.

21. Jung, CW8: 131.

22. Jung, CW8: 251.

23. Hillman, Insearch: Psychology and Religion, 38.

24. Jung, CW8: 174.

25. Wolfgang Geigerich, The Soul's Logical Life, 114.

26. Ibid, 93.

27. Jung, CW8: 177.

28. Geigerich, 34.

29. Ibid, 146.

30. Jung, CW8: 177.

31. Geigerich, 274.

32. Jung, CW7: 71.

33. Geigerich, 274.

34. Hillman, Healing Fiction, 95.

35. Jung, CW9i: 91.

36. Hawkings, 175.

37. Jung, CW5: 551.

Preparation for the Journey

To change what ails the world of business will take time. There are no magic pills to swallow, no quick and easy fixes. A marketing manager will not help you if you do not know your own story. There is nothing to market and you waste valuable organizational resources that could be spent on developing your leaders, both young and old. Without a story in which your archetypal values live and continually breathe, it is impossible to brand your organization, for you cannot brand something that doesn't exist. You will have empty words with no meaning and worse, alienate the very employees you are trying to retain.

To renew the foundation on which your career was first built will provide a strong foundation on which to build for the future. If you choose your attitude to be fearless, to pursue excellence in your own life work and not look without to those who serve a salary not a profession, you will find resources that will not be available to any other. Find your allies and let the non-believers fight amongst themselves. Find your tribe…those that share your values and your beliefs. It is with your tribe that you share your life work and your clients. The pretenders will fall away as they have an inability to form an authentic relationship. Reclaim your passion for your life work, your love for your chosen field of practice. Renew your relationship.

When you have done all of this, then you will have something worth branding. For branding comes from archetypal psychology—the study of relationships and their meaning. True branding rests on recognition of an archetype and an archetype always demands authenticity. To use a mythic approach to your life work, directs the mind and heart to the ultimate mystery that contains all existence. To use a mythic approach enables you to see what is just beyond your field of sight, to re-vision your relationship both personally and professionally. "Live" Nietzsche says "as though the day were here." Each individual must claim the power of his or her Heroic Journey. A mythic imagination can lead the way forward. How?

This mythoi or little story, comes from the Grail. The Grail is the only myth where the heroic deed is an act of speech, so perhaps a fitting one for the problem at hand in finding an authentic voice.

The knight, Gawain, and the boys were out hunting. They had caught much game and wanted to make camp for the night and cook their dinner. They needed water for the cooking pots and one of the hunters said that he had spotted a well a little ways back in the forest. He volunteered to go fetch water for cooking and sauntered off.

As he approached the well, a hideous creature appeared before him. She was the ugliest, smelliest, wartiest, most disgusting creature he had ever the misfortune to lay eyes upon. She jumped in front of the well and demanded, "What do you want?" He replied, "If you please, I have come for water." She nodded. "Water you may have, but first you must kiss me." Horrified at this request, the hunter ran back to the group and told his tale of woe. The other hunters laughed at his discomfort and several others also made the attempt but with no success. The creature truly was terrible to behold and her request unbearable to contemplate.

Gawain in disgust watched his hunters fail repeatedly. Finally, he said, "I am a Knight. I will go and face this creature and get the water we need." He proceeded off into the forest and approached the well. Sure enough, the hag appeared. She jumped in front of the well and demanded, "What do you want?" He replied, "If you please, I have come for water." She nodded. "Water you may have, but first you must kiss me." Gawain did, and I must add, did a quite a thorough job indeed.

As you might have anticipated, for this is truly a myth, the hag then turned into the most exquisite beauty he had ever seen. She smiled and said "You have won me by deed (which was the way of the times) now choose. Do you wish my current shape for your pleasure at night and my other shape for your friends to admire during the day? Or, my current shape for your friends to envy and my other shape for your pleasure at night?" Gawain did not hesitate for he was a true Knight. "My lady, the choice must be yours," he said, "for it is your body." She smiled sweetly again and stated. "Dear Knight, you have not only named my heart's desire, but the desire of any of us. To hold the power to choose."

To follow your bliss, you must claim your power to choose. Such an act involves risk, as you then become vulnerable to loss. Your choice might be refused. Your choice may be ridiculed. But, if you do not make it, you lose passion for your life work. You may lose the passion for your life. Thus the importance of the Heroic Journey, as it provides a working map for the territory of choice.

Never forget you have the power to choose. Choose your life. Pack light for the journey. Take a long look at yourself in the mirror. To embark on your own Heroic Journey is to embark on a path that will forever change you. Surrender your old life and walk towards the future. Live your life as a work of art. Ready?

Let us begin.

The Heroic Journey

Importance of Individual Recognition, Relationship and Meaning in order to achieve Corporate Alignment, Integration and Engagement

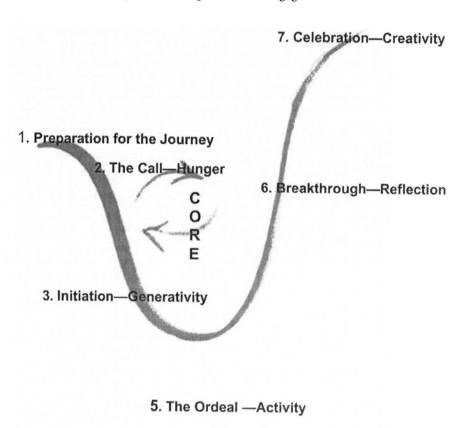

The Call—Hunger

The power of story has always had the capacity to nourish the human soul. With the corporate world in a state of turmoil and some believe disintegration of old paradigms resulting from illegal actions taken by corporations such as Enron, Tyco, Mediacom, Arthur Anderson, and others, according to Joel Bakan in his recent work *The Corporation,* some organizations have even been diagnosed as pathological. There is a method that allows one to move away from Bakan's pathological corporate stance and provide an alternate perspective through which to view a corporate environment, one that nourishes the workers within the corporation and the external community without. This approach attempts to discover in an organizational environment the stories that nourish human beings, individually and collectively. Here, theory and practice must reinforce each other. Archetypal psychology, with its foundation in multiplicity, can provide a foundation for such an approach. In order to reawaken the originating principles of any organization, one should remember that those very principles came from individuals. In other words, the *stories* of those individuals formed the genesis or *archai* of the organization. In order to brand your organization, you need to know your own story.

As human beings individuate, the concept of Self must necessarily extend beyond a singular identity and explore an interconnectedness with others, with the environment, with communities, and even with nations. One form of interconnectedness takes the shape of the modern corporation where a group of like-minded individuals pursue a common vision. If organizations and the people within them are suffering, one could assume that the origin of such suffering is a hunger for change. If work is the predominant activity in people's lives, it is also reasonable to assume that many individuals will long for, or hunger for "work" that has meaning.

Some critics might argue that the current condition of most corporations does not serve society; but instead causes harm to both workers and the community. The field of *change management* in today's organizational setting addresses ways in which an organization can transform its internal environment, or corporate culture, to set a new direction for the organization as a whole. If newspaper articles and editorials are to be believed, such a transformation is sorely needed, yet current corporate practices suggest that most approaches at change management fail.

For years, corporations have dealt with growing competition by introducing so-called "improvements" into every function and process. But competitive pressure is increasing, forcing corporations to search for higher levels of quality and service to maintain overall market agility. The treadmill keeps moving faster as corporations push employees to work harder, often with modest or no results and with increased stress and suffering for the employees.

One problem seems to be that too few people at every level support the change initiative at an *emotional* level. To foster imagination and proactive effort, emotional commitment is required. Change is a psychological event, not a logical one. Since change is experienced on a personal level, each employee must think and feel differently. Leaders must engage with all of their employees. For new information to flow across organizational boundaries, the old top-down, hierarchical approach seems counter-productive if not outmoded. In managing change in a fast-paced environment, the challenge is to balance all of the pieces of the organizational puzzle and to recognize that such change reflects a dynamic, living process. But how is an organization transformed? The answer can only be: *one person at a time.* Individual development must act as a mirror image to the development of the organization as a whole.

Demographics are also changing. A *Harvard Business Review* article reports that the Bureau of Labor Statistics projects a shortfall of 10 million workers in the United States in 2010. The authors expand on the demographic:

> The problem will not simply be a lack of able bodies but rather the skills, knowledge, experience, and relationships that walk out the door every time somebody retires—and they take time and money to replace. Given the inevitable time lag between the demand for skills and the ability of the educational system to provide them, we'll see a particularly pronounced skill shortage in fast-growing technical fields such as health care. What's more, employees are your face to the marketplace. It's good business to have employees who reflect the ethnic, gender, and yes, age composition of your customer base—especially when those customers are well-off. Baby boomers will be the most financially powerful generation of mature consumers ever; today's mature adults control more than $7 trillion in wealth in the United States—70% of the total.[1]

The currency of a knowledge economy is, of course, learning—the continuation of knowledge. In order for any organization to attract and keep valuable knowledge workers, personal and professional development should become its high priority.

An invitation to such personal and professional development begins with what Joseph Campbell, drawing on patterns in world mythologies, termed *The Call*. This might occur in a situation of dissatisfaction with a job or a relationship. This call for change might begin loud and clear or it might appear less obviously as a persistent nagging that something is wrong. This book will show how to extend Campbell's work into a corporate environment and explore the model of the Heroic Journey, and how it might provide a mythic map for corporate change. The goal will be a framework for the creation of a corporate culture that inspires and maintains ongoing dialogue between the people who instigate new strategies and those who are expected to carry them out. Whatever form change takes, the journey begins with a desire to expand into something more; the courage to abdicate the familiar and the fortitude to set off on a quest. My work will use Jung's metamythology as a guidepost to illustrate the inner journey that necessarily precedes an act of outward innovation.

I will explore the notion of psychic hunger as a crucial component to personal and corporate change. Where does psychic hunger originate, and what impact does it have on an individual or on an organization? What impetus has fueled the creation of a corporation? Who gave birth to it? If the founder is still present and active in the organization, a different set of questions arises than if another executive now leads the company. The corporate mythology (the original bundle of inspired values and beliefs) will also shapeshift if a merger or acquisition has taken place, causing two or more mythologies to collide. Do they blend? Is one assimilated?

To find this original mythos is not a simple task, since a psychic drive is located, according to archetypal theory, in the unconscious depths and sets the foundation on which individual personality is constructed. Since an organization is a collection of individuals, the foundation of the organization becomes exponentially more complex. In terms of hunger, a physical hunger can be satisfied by the consumption of food. A psychic hunger requires a different form of nourishment. Jung explains:

> *Hunger*, as a characteristic expression of the instinct of self-preservation, is without a doubt one of the primary and most powerful factors influencing behavior; in fact, the lives of primitives are more strongly affected by it than by sexuality. At this level, hunger is the alpha and omega—existence itself.[2]

A key factor to note in Jung's explanation is the act of self-preservation. To reach beyond current circumstance and move towards an unknown future requires a core foundation that will support ambiguity. A return to the image that generated the foundation is necessary. Archetypes are the invisible support for the image or vision that provided the original impetus for the journey. To access the archetype, an archetypal image is required. Jung explains that

> archetypes are not determined as regards their content, but only as regards their form and then only to a very limited degree. A primordial image is determined as to its content only when it has become conscious and is therefore filled out with the material of conscious experience. [3]

If an image exemplifying psychic hunger can be located in the experience of a conscious individual, this image can then serve to represent the concrete manifestation of such hunger. The interplay between the individual and his or her environment, the organization, will potentially expand the meaning associated with the image. Thus, the image begins to act as a foundation or as a catalyst that initiates language capable of deepening the experience.

My experience as a consultant has allowed me to use image to access "hunger" that has not yet been expressed in language. The process I use provides access, through image, to beliefs and desires that are not consciously available to the individual and therefore to the organization. Using an image or a series of images permits access to the language of metaphor that can shed light on what is hidden from view, the invisible aspects of a corporate culture that can block or impede an act of creativity that necessarily precedes innovation.

These metaphors represent a concrete reality that constructs a living mythology. As Hillman claims, "the curious difficulty of explaining just what archetypes are suggest something specific to them. That is, they tend to be metaphors rather than things."[4] Metaphors take on life in the stories told about an individual skill or group collaboration. Narratives that represent the narrative extension of a metaphor or image then becomes a trajectory for future action. To look at the metaphors operational within a corporation allows for an "under-standing" of the corporate mythology, a glimpse into what stands under and supports behavior.

Joseph Campbell's mythic pattern can offer new insight by probing the archetypal narratives living within organizations. Campbell explored this concept of the Heroic Journey, which can be utilized as an analogy to Jung's process of individuation, because any deviation from the cultural norm presents a risk for the individual. According to Campbell,

Throughout the inhabited world, in all times and under every circumstance, the myths of man have flourished; and they have been the living inspiration of whatever else may have appeared out of the activities of the human body and mind. It would not be too much to say that myth is the secret opening through which the inexhaustible energies of the cosmos pour into human cultural manifestation.[5]

Campbell further explains: "in the absence of an effective general mythology, each of us has his private, unrecognized, rudimentary, yet secretly potent pantheon of dream."[6] Out of such a dream or vision come the ideas that drive a desire to create something new or different, to make one's mark upon the world. If formally or organized according to legal requirements, we call such a community of like-minded individuals a corporation. When this individual dream or vision is shared with others, it forms a living entity called a "mythology," and as such, is capable of inspiring others who also share the same beliefs or values to action.

Campbell suggests that "it has always been the prime function of mythology and rite to supply the symbols that carry the human spirit forward, in counteraction to those other constant human fantasies that tend to tie it back."[7] In corporate life, when any individual or a group of individuals desires to create something new, opposition can be the first response to change. Change is a painful process, and yet if any organization is to be successful, it must master change as well as maintain the core vision that inspired its creation. If the organization has not created a psychic space for creation of new ideas, it is not unusual for a pioneer to leave that organization and head out alone. Such is the nature of what Campbell refers to as "the Call." The idea or vision is so powerful that the individual feels compelled to follow the inner voice that is leading onward, to appease his or her psychic hunger, no matter the response from the status quo.

Digging through the massive amounts of organizational and leadership development literature and my experience as a consultant has led me to propose that Campbell's idea of the "Call" and Jung's idea of "hunger" may be analogous, if not the same, and that the presence of such an impetus is required in order to move the individual forward into the unknown. But the individual responding to the Call is not necessarily alone, as Campbell reminds us:

[…] We have not even to risk the adventure alone; for the heroes of all time have gone before us; the labyrinth is thoroughly known; we have only to follow the thread of the hero-path. And where we had thought to find an abomination, we shall find a god; where we had thought to slay another, we shall slay ourselves; where we had thought to travel outward, we shall come to the center of our own existence; where we had thought to be alone, we shall be with all the world.[8]

Campbell links the journey of the individual to that of every heroic journey throughout the ages, providing a psychological guide for the process. Since our source of economic power arguably resides in people, a framework for the individual journey is needed. Peter Drucker, through his analysis of today's "knowledge economy," is a leading proponent of this view. "The basic economic resources—'the means of production', to use the economist's term is no longer capital, nor natural resources [...] not 'labor.' It is and will be knowledge."[9] Assets now have feet. For a corporation to succeed, the organization relies on the ideas of individual members. If a given idea survives the tests of applicability, the individual brings it back into his or her community once more. In a knowledge-based economy, collaboration becomes imperative for success, rendering the hunger for self-preservation both an individual and a tribal concern.

A corporation that wishes to survive will need to address the story of each individual and attempt to integrate the belief system of each of them with the belief system of the organization. Today with such a diverse and multi-generational network of knowledge workers, a living, working mythology is required that provides a safe container for both individual and corporation. An archetypal approach can assist in defining a working mythology capable of handling such complexity.

What drives an individual to follow an unknown path? When an individual is motivated by "hunger" for something that has not been named, only an act of creation can satisfy it. A corporation is no exception for as it fights for market share, it believes in much the same way as a tribe fighting for its existence. As a group of individuals sharing the same desire grows, Schein, in *Organizational Culture*, claims that two other factors come into play:

> All group and organizational theories distinguish two major sets of problems that all groups, no matter what their size, must deal with: (1) survival, growth, and adaptation in their environment and (2) internal integration that permits daily functioning and the ability to adapt.[10]

The locus of control being either external or internal demands a *both/and* approach as opposed to choosing one set of metaphors over the other. This *both/and* approach is meant to hold the tension between external growth and adaptation and internal integration, or as Jung named this condition, "a tension of the opposites."[11] This is the tension created by Collins and Porras through "preserving the core" *and* "stimulate progress."

Traditional approaches to managing an organization have been primarily one-sided, giving primacy to one mode of operation over another. For example, a manager may focus on bottom-line profit or on growth, but the approach is unable to hold the concept of both. A management style needs to be constructed to incorporate both loci of control and must be capable of holding a circular focus as questions of survival, growth, and adaptation will impact internal integration, and vice-versa. Such a management style provides the foundation for the transcendent function in that the tension held between the opposites creates a space in which creativity can flourish and function.

When complexity is the norm, any attempts at simplification will provide only a superficial method of management and limited success. Looking inward and outward at the same time is necessary if any individual is to both evaluate and change any organizational environment. A focus of *both/and* provides a guide for behavior. Schein elaborates further:

> Overt behavior is always determined both by the culture predisposition (the perceptions, thoughts, and feelings that are patterned) and by the situational contingencies that arise from the immediate external environment.[12]

In order to evaluate any situational contingency, an individual belief system must be clarified. Such a belief system can be seen as a personal mythology, a living pattern of beliefs that acts as a guide. One of the main functions of a living mythology is to provide a container for interaction between internal and external events. Such a container is organic, one that is ever-growing and adapting. This is why a start-up organization is sometimes called an "incubator," linking the idea of how medicine protects a newborn child with how the business world protects a developing idea. In an incubator environment, those shared sets of basic assumptions of individuals will grow and expand into a new corporation. How does this shared set of assumptions take form?

When basic assumptions have been codified as corporate vision, a structure is established that provides a foundation for future growth while at the same time holding fast the core ideology that motivates the construction of such a structure in the first place. Schein elaborates on this aspect of a newly forming group of individuals who hold a common vision:

One of these elements is that culture implies some level of *structural stability* in the group. When we say that something is "cultural," we imply that it is not only shared but deep and stable. By deep I mean less conscious and therefore less tangible and less visible. The other element that lends stability is *patterning or integration* of the elements into a larger paradigm or gestalt that ties together the various elements and that lies at a deeper level. Culture somehow implies that rituals, climate, values, and behaviors bind together into a coherent whole. This patterning or integration is the *essence* of what we mean by "culture." [13]

Thus, if an individual has discovered a hunger for something he or she cannot yet express, how can its essence be defined? A return to the unconscious content of an individual psyche may provide an answer. As Jung so often claimed, the problem with the unconscious is that it is unconscious and as such, it has yet to be understood, or expressed. Schein concurs and states in reference to individuals within organizations: "They cannot tell you what their culture is, any more than fish, if they could talk, could tell you what water is."[14] If the patterns evident in either an individual or an organization are viewed with this idea of structural stability, such conceptual paradigms can be made more concrete and therefore visible.

The fundamental desires of any individual can be classified into three main goals whose consequence is individual and structural stability. Such goals are *relationship, recognition,* and *meaning.* If the unconscious of an individual is considered, which, as the group of individuals expands, will become the unconscious content of the group or collective, such unconscious content holds the key to understanding the shared "mental models" of an organization. Schein agrees and adds:

The implications of this way of thinking about culture are profound. For one thing, you begin to realize that culture is so stable and difficult to change because it represents the accumulated learning of a group—the ways of thinking, feeling and perceiving the world that have made the group successful. For another thing, you realize that the important parts of culture are essentially invisible. Culture at this deeper level can be thought of as the shared mental models that the members of an organization hold and take for granted.[15]

In order to make these mental models visible, one needs an understanding of the framework within the organization itself. To arrive at such a framework, it is necessary to question the original framework that individuals bring to an organization. Such individual framework taken collectively provides the culture in which all participants reside. The strands of that framework are woven from the foundational aspects of a living mythology, namely recognition, relationship and meaning.

The Call for Recognition

The old-style management of command and control that seems to have been borrowed from the military is no longer functional and, in fact, may now prove detrimental to the success of an organization. Schein makes a very provocative observation when he suggests "much of what we call today command-and-control systems have at their root the assumption that employees cannot be trusted."[16] If there is a psychic hunger for recognition in an individual, and he or she is living and working in an environment based on mistrust, this hunger will not be fed. Each person knows, at some level, that there is more to life than mere survival. Those that find their Call early in life are most fortunate. Others come to their Call later in life. Jung referred to this path as individuation. Each person is capable of a meaningful life, but to choose such a path actively is to respond to a Call. The path of authenticity thus allows each individual to discover and explore this age-old mystery. As Jung so often states, we are driven to be ourselves, the individual "becomes what he always was."[17]

If an organization does not recognize this need in each person, it ignores what is arguably one of the greatest motivators known throughout history: the belief system of an individual that comes from the archetypal depths of the psyche. Jung called such a system of beliefs "archetypes of transformation." He elaborates:

> They are not personalities, but are typical situations, places, ways and means, that symbolize the kind of transformation in question. Like the personalities, these archetypes are true and genuine symbols that cannot be exhaustively interpreted, either as signs or as allegories.[18]

In other words, the belief or value system of an individual contains "ground principles, the άρχαί of the unconscious and are indescribable because of their wealth of reference, although in themselves recognizable."[19] These ground principles or values can be expressed in the belief system held by an individual. To bring these ground principles into conscious awareness enables a group of individuals to align common ground principles. Such common ground is the mythology of the corporation itself. These archetypes of transformation can act as an impetus to allow either an individual or a group of like-minded individuals to transform a previous mind-set into a new framework that feeds psychic hunger, and accepts the Call.

The Call to Relationship

In order to explore what constitutes a Call in the context of relationship, a relationship must be understood as having two parts: with self and with others. Campbell and Jung both believed that most people are imprisoned within lives that are too small. The limitless potential of childhood has been replaced with the difficulty of life itself encompassing so many variables that prevent the individual from hearing a Call to a greater adventure. Part of the difficulty in following a Call to a larger life is the individual's fear of the unknown. If the Call is followed, stability that has previously been so carefully created by the individual will be shaken, perhaps changed or destroyed forever. Jung continues to focus on the positive aspects of change when he states: "Whatever the nature of the psyche may be, it is endowed with an extraordinary capacity for variation and transformation."[20]

To follow this Call takes great courage; to ignore a Call can cause psychic pain and a diminished life. Jung maintains that the cause of neurotic behavior is compensatory, an attempt of the self-regulating psychic system to restore balance from within. [21] This is a move towards a more spiritual life, one that meets the secrets and mysteries of existence, while at the same time, celebrating individual uniqueness in each person's way of belonging to the world. Everyone, to some extent, backs away from personal authenticity. To live an authentic life requires each individual to reach beyond what is immediately at hand, to reach towards the potential inherent in each child, perhaps to return to a childlike-state of innocence when fear is not such a factor in the consideration of options. To live an authentic life means not settling for what is easily available but to remain linked to that mystery of life, however culturally expressed or defined. When society supports such individual uniqueness, there are infinite ways to express an innate hunger.

> It is not only that we use the word hunger in different senses, but in combination with other factors hunger can assume the most varied forms. The originally simple and unequivocal determinant can appear transformed into pure greed, or into many aspects of boundless desire or insatiability, as for instance the lust for gain or inordinate ambition.[22]

There is ample evidence that points to the greed that overtakes some organizations and seems to be a hallmark of command-control environments. But such emphasis on the bottom-line of profit damages the relationship between the organization and its workers. This notion has been well captured by Deal and Kennedy in *The New Corporate Cultures:* "virtually all cost-cutting undertaken by companies has seriously weakened their cultural cohesion."[23]. They offer a poignant example:

> In 1995, a year in which large companies laid off 440,000 employees, the average salary of their CEO's increased by 18%, to just over $1.6 million. Including long-term incentives such as stock options, average CEO total pay increased 30%, to $3.7 million.[24]

In an environment characterized by greed, it is almost impossible for the front-line employees to believe in the direction and vision of the organization. In such a situation, work becomes *just a job* undertaken only for survival. This type of atmosphere creates an environment that promotes selfish, short-term thinking and behaviors that do not support long-term innovation. There is no "community" of belief that supports the organization moving onward. In his ongoing work, Schein examines how a community organizes itself. Is it around the individual or organized around a group? Schein asks a pivotal question: "If the individual's interests and those of the community (country) are in conflict, who is expected to make the sacrifice?"[25] What kind of culture might support a Call to change and how would it do so?

James Hillman presents an additional perspective. In his book *Insearch: Psychology and Religion*, he states that "need makes us human; if we did not need one another, if we could meet and satisfy our own needs, there would be no human society."[26] To identify a psychic need is to identify a psychic "hunger"; when such realization takes place, it is here that the foundation of the Call rests. If the community at hand will not support the Call received by an individual, then certain individuals will be forced to search for a new community.

What attributes are clearly evident in an organization, or what methods or procedures are in place that address the need for relationship? Does the corporate culture support this innate need? In the section on "So How Does it Work", practical examples will be given.

The Call to Meaning

The culture of any organization is the web of beliefs and values, the rituals and stories that create meaning for the people within the organization. This web is a living mythology that can be fed and, if consciously nourished, assists in ensuring that the organization and its people will remain psychologically healthy. As Nobel Prize-winning economist Robert Fogel comments:

> Today, people are increasingly concerned with what life is all about. That was not true for the ordinary individual in 1885 when nearly the whole day was devoted to earning the food, clothing and shelter needed to sustain life.[27]

What really drives the culture—its essence or quiddity—is the consistency of the values that are expressed by the day-to-day behavior of the workers within it. Those values, if clearly defined and repeatedly articulated, provide a common meaning to members of the organization. Each member follows his or her own Heroic Journey within the context of the organization that is also following a Heroic Journey. An archetypal approach, using a conscious mythology as a mode of knowing, permits both individual and collective individuation. This way of thinking defines leadership as something each individual can realize. Leadership becomes context dependent and supported by a cohesive organizational culture that encourages each member to participate in individuation, or in organizational terms, in professional and personal development. Deal and Kennedy write:

> But it is not just the leadership that allows the company to carry out its economic mission successfully. It is leadership that seeks to shape a working environment that people at all levels can identify with. It is leadership that encourages leadership from everyone. It is leadership that is not afraid to stand for something. It is leadership that cares about a myriad of details that make the company work. It is leadership that strives to generate universal pride in what the company accomplishes, not just how people are enriched by its economic activities. It is leadership that all good managers should exercise if they take themselves and their responsibilities seriously.[28]

To return to the ground principles that both inspire and motivate human endeavor and recognize that those ground principles are dynamic in expression permits both individual and organizational flexibility. There is no one single but many right answers. A return to those archetypal ground principles provides a firm foundation on which innovation can be seeded and grow.

So How Does it Work?

How might the concepts of relationship, recognition, and meaning be put into practice?

A specific example comes from a small credit union in British Columbia called Envision Financial. CEO, Gord Huston, provides a little historical background.

> Envision was created January 2001 as result of the merger of First Heritage Savings Credit Union and Delta Credit Union. Both organizations were formed in the 1940's and had a proud and successful history, and significantly different cultures. Envision has been very successful, in fact, more successful than the momentum of the founding credit unions. This success is true in financial terms as well as employee and member-owner satisfaction levels. What caused this to happen? Simply that the 700 plus people who chose Envision as a place to work got behind our Vision and made it happen. I was smart enough to realize that one of the main things I could do was to get out of the way.

And in reference to what precipitated a Call to creating their own university and educational programs, Huston states:

> The call came mainly through the Vision of one of our staff members (Carol Hama), who saw that the conventional methods of investing in staff at financial institutions was not relevant to the needs of our people. Many people had received their high school diplomas and entered the workforce, while maintaining a strong desire to develop academically and professionally. EnvisionU was created to meet this need and create a win-win for the organization and the staff members. Visions like this require a commitment of resources as well as time, money and Executive support. Fortunately, Envision's culture is open to innovative ideas and we know that investment in people is critical to our future success. Having said that, this innovation made it due to the fact that the idea was championed by a passionate person who ensured it made through the gauntlet of cost cutting to become a reality.

I will follow the story of Envision throughout the following chapters as they provide a great example of tapping the hidden potential within an organization. To realize that each employee has ability beyond a job description is the hallmark of a great organization. Gord Huston acted on this knowledge and championed the project. More detail will be provided in the next chapter on Initiation—Generativity.

The following are additional examples, merged from several organizations, of the dynamics of building a team with these concepts in mind. I have purposely mixed responses from organizations in order to protect the identity of any individual or specific organization.

In these examples, I was asked to provide the foundation by which a team could be constructed. It was to be involved in new product design, so trust among its members was critical. The team consisted of expert engineers and software designers, ranging in ages from early twenties to early sixties and was culturally diverse, with people from countries around the world. They had never before worked together so achieving some kind of cohesion was a desired outcome.

The team mandate was to create a mission statement. Traditionally, mission statements consist of three parts: who you are, what you do, and for whom. Instead of resorting to language to create the mission statement, I asked the team members to choose an image that represented who they were and what they brought to the team.[29] The images consisted of several hundred postcards ranging from many images such as sculptures, works of art, or landscapes. Each individual was asked to speak to the chosen image and provide an explanation as to how his or her image could be linked to the other team members. The linkage could be anything, in terms of color, shape, experience, history, or location. The idea was to have them use their imaginations rather than logic for this connection.

The process allowed a relationship to emerge quite different from what this group would encounter in a normal workday. Each individual brought a story to the image, providing personal information that otherwise might not have been revealed. These images provided a way to deepen relationships, allowing each participant to access a source that was not superficial, as in the case of a usual business persona. I envisioned the mythological figure of Psyche entering this workspace to provide a new vehicle for language. This approach also permitted the Heroic Journey to enter as a mythological model represented by each participant and his or her individual story. By linking each image and story with the next image and story, a shared story began to take form. Each person named and then publicly claimed the individual "Call" which brought him or her to the team.

Each participant now had an image representing who he or she was as a complete individual, a much fuller state of being than just a business persona. The next step was to identify the archetypal ground principles or core values that each member brought to the endeavor. They were all given an assortment of index cards on which were written potential archetypes of transformation represented by values such as "safety," "family" or "creativity." They were then asked to write a description of that particular value. Each person shared his or her description and a list of descriptors was place under each term. The team then discussed which descriptors best represented a collective understanding of the term, a heated process that took several hours. At the end of the session, a common language had been developed whereby the team could align its work ethos and provide space for each participant to follow his or her individual Call. It was decided to allow the experience to deepen and see what would develop.

One month later I returned for another session. In the intervening time, the team had decided that they would not formally articulate their mission statement in language but instead remain with the images that represented who they were as individuals. An intranet site had been developed where the images had been digitized. To click on any image would produce a picture of the individual, a biography of relevant work experience, and a small story describing each Call. The images had been literally linked together using the image of a link to attach each image to the other. The team had also digitized the descriptors of their commonly held values and constructed a white board that could be used to display them in a flexible setting. Each descriptor had been magnetized, allowing the values to be sorted in a multitude of ways since each project or design implementation would require a different value to take priority. As circumstances arising within an organizational setting are context-dependent, the inherent flexibility in holding multiple values could permit many approaches to be considered without deviation from the established core. The team had decided that this was the best way to describe themselves collectively to prevent their shared value system from becoming rigid by fixed, literally immovable definition.

The second process was for each team member to construct a Touchstone.[30] The Touchstone would be built using various art materials such as plasticene, miscellaneous toys, natural materials such as twigs, branches, leaves, or moss, construction paper, lego, nuts, bolts, and any other materials that had been collected that held meaning to the participant. Each team member worked for several hours, and then when each work of art was completed, offered a story—a mythos—that described the Touchstone. Each participant linked his or her story and Touchstone to other participants, eventually forming one large work of Art.

At the end of the process, the team had assembled both a shared story and a shared representation that could collectively hold it. It was decided that the Touchstone would be then be photographed and digitized in order to construct a large image that could be displayed. If any team member left this particular team, his or her contribution would remain as a visual image thus linking the team forever. Any new member, as an initiation into the team, would be asked to repeat the process, thus building a living mythology that would provide recognition of each member and their contribution, describe the relationship between the members and allow for shared meaning that could grow with the team.

It was also decided to create from patio blocks or stones a pathway that led to the building that housed the team. Each patio stone would have on its face one of the words identifying the value system of the team. The rest of the organization would then literally walk upon the foundation that held this particular team and at the same time, both have an experience of the common ground and learn the value system without resorting to language. The images provided the mission statement and an experience of what that mission statement meant to the team.

Working in such an archetypal framework permitted these participants to construct a shared meaning, which held both individual and collective significance.

Notes: The Call

1. Dychtwald, Erickson, and Morison, Harvard Business Review 2004, 2.

2. Jung, CW8: 237.

3. Jung, CW9i: 155.

4. Hillman, Re-Visioning Psychology, xiii.

5. Campbell, The Hero With a Thousand Faces, 3.

6. Ibid, 4.

7. Ibid, 11.

8. Ibid, 25.

9. Drucker, The Essential Drucker, 8.

10. Edgar Schein, Organizational Culture, 11.

11. Jung, CW8: 189.

12. Schein, Organizational Culture and Leadership, 14.

13. Ibid, 10.

14. Schein, The Corporate Culture Survival Guide, 21.

15. Ibid, 21.

16. Ibid, 51.

17. Jung, CW9i: 84.

18. Jung, CW9i: 80.

19. Ibid.

20. Jung, CW8: 235.

21. Jung, CW18: 389.

22. Jung, CW8: 236.

23. Deal and Kennedy, The New Corporate Cultures, 63. Deal and Kennedy have written extensively on the importance of corporate cultures and both the original book and this revised edition are an excellent introduction to the care and feeding of any corporate culture.

24. Ibid, 73.

25. Schein, The Corporate Culture Survival Guide, 52.

26. Hillman, Insearch: Psychology and Religion, 18.

27. Fogel, The Fourth Great Awakening and the Future of Egalitarianism, 19.

28. Deal and Kennedy, 37.

29. Personal conversations with consultants Cheryl De Ciantis and Kenton Hyatt, January 2003. This process was originally devised by Cheryl De Ciantis (see article below) and it is one of my favourite tools in using an archetypal approach in organizations. My postcard collection is about 4,000 strong in number and still growing. It gives me something to do while waiting in airports!

30. De Ciantis, Cheryl. "What Does Drawing My Hand Have to Do with Leadership?", 88.

Initiation—Generativity

To continue working within the image provided by the Heroic Journey, initiation is the next phase in the process. Initiation is an integral part of life, whether personal or professional. Initiation ceremonies or rites of passage were very common historically, but unfortunately, such rites of passage are not common today.

To *initiate*, borrowed from the Latin *initiāre*, meaning "to begin" or "originate," is commonly to introduce or commence some knowledge or practice.[1] In Jung's drive model, sexuality is the next drive that manifests itself in the psychic structure, and I will compare this drive as an energy force that originates or begins an act, providing a parallel to initiation in the Heroic Journey.

How does initiation, as a beginning or an act of beginning, affect a corporate entity? Management must build an environment that perpetuates the organization. Through its leadership and succession planning, an organization is generative, or is ideally meant to be.

In many professions such as medicine, law, and accounting, initiation still plays an important role in organizational life. There is a period of initiation before full acceptance as a member of the profession is awarded to the individual. When an individual first joins an organization, he or she experiences rites of passage, whether explicit or implicit, which play a part in initiating the new employee. If one views initiation as a creative act meant to be generative, to bring the individual forward into something new or different, then an act of initiation becomes an act of creative power. Jung illustrates such a quality:

> The conflict between ethics and sex today is not just a collision between instinctuality and morality, but a struggle to give an instinct its rightful place in our lives, and to recognize in this instinct a power which seeks expression and evidently may not be trifled with, and therefore cannot be made to fit in with our well-meaning moral laws. Sexuality is not mere instinctuality; it is an indisputably creative power that is not only the basic cause of our individual lives, but a very serious factor in our psychic life as well.[2]

The sexual instinct as a creative power or generative function is complex. The combinations of a generative function and aspects of emotion, further combining with material interests, have become problematic. It is not necessary to elaborate further a rampant corporate greed that permeates the media. In most organizations today, the environment is often toxic at its best, and pathological at its worst. If the shift from the old industrial paradigm has not been made to the new knowledge paradigm, toxicity can become rampant. In the movie *The Corporation*, Joel Bakan provides the following list of symptoms observed in some organizations:

1.   a failure to comply with social norms with respect to lawful behaviors

2.   reckless disregard for the safety of others

3.   deceitfulness: repeated lying or conning others for profit

4.   callous unconcern for the feelings of others; and

5.   incapacity to experience guilt.

These attributes are symptomatic of psychopathic behavior. Although Bakan's work is intended to shock, even to antagonize, it is conceivable that his work be considered a "Call." One-sided in the extreme, yes, but viewed from the angle of a Call to action, it may produce enough emotional impetus to produce change. Such a view may be naïve or idealistic; but if corporations are to improve their image, some changes are necessary. If a more conscious view is needed to address the ramifications of corporate behavior, then Bakan's work has fulfilled such a need. If an individual is motivated to instigate change as a result of such blatant bias, Bakan will have fulfilled his objective in stirring the collective organizational psyche. A word of caution is needed, however, for when unconscious contents are stimulated, it is foolhardy to assume that the unconscious is an area of psyche that is controllable.

If historical antecedents are examined, one soon discovers that the corporation as an entity has been suspect since its inception into social life. In his historical review, Bakan states:

> Businessmen and politicians had been suspicious of the corporation from the time it first emerged in the late sixteenth century. Unlike the prevailing partnership form, in which relatively small groups of men, bonded together by personal loyalties and mutual trust, pooled their resources to set up businesses

they ran as well as owned, the corporation separated ownership from management—one group of people, directors and managers, ran the firm, while
another group, shareholders, owned it. That unique design was believed by
many to be a recipe for corruption and scandal. [3]

The design that separates ownership from management can be examined by
returning to aspects of relationship, recognition, and meaning. In these three crucial areas, most current organizations fail miserably. Emphasis on the bottom line
of profitability only, eliminates the need for recognition as the organization does
not recognize the value of individual members, destroys relationships as the need
for power predominates, and reduces the search for meaning to pure profit only.
In the meta-analysis conducted by the Gallup organization, it was found that
"employee perceptions of quality of management practices measured by the 13
Core items are related to business unit outcomes" and that "the validity of
employee perceptions of quality of management practices measured by the 13
Core items generalizes across the organizations studied."[4] In brief, the more positive the results of the 13 Core items, the better the performance of the business
unit. A meta-analysis was used in order to provide a statistical integration of data
across various studies. To support the use of this method, the authors claim that

> meta-analysis eliminates biases and provides an estimate of true validity or true
> relationship between two or more variables. Statistics typically calculated dur-
> ing meta-analyses also allow the researcher to explore the presence, or lack
> thereof, of moderators of relationships. [...] It provides a method by which
> researchers can ascertain whether validities and relationships generalize across
> various situations (e.g., across firms or geographical locations). [5]

In order to shift into a new paradigm, agents of change within an organization
are needed to examine these relationships and make a potentially pathological,
unconscious condition conscious. In a therapeutic sense, if awareness of the damaging behavior becomes conscious to a psychopathic or narcissistic personality,
treatment is completed. For a narcissist, conscious ownership of the damaging
behavior is a therapeutic breakthrough, the pattern of narcissism has been broken.

If conscious recognition is given to the environment, it is perceived through
the senses. That apperception of place, of location is unconsciously affected by
the environment in which we find ourselves. Jung also emphasized the archetype
of "place" as one that has transformational power.[6] To recognize what motivates

an individual will also inform the type of surroundings necessary to enhance performance.

Hillman remarks:

> Because our psychic stuff is images, image-making is a *via regia*, a royal road to soul-making. The making of soul-stuff calls for dreaming, fantasying, imagining. To live psychologically means to imagine things; to be in touch with soul means to live in sensuous connection with fantasy. To be in soul is to experience the fantasy in all realities and the basic reality of fantasy.[7]

To ask questions in this "realm of fantasy" and to explore the potential interactions between reality and fantasy, provide many alternatives that can be explored by the employees. This tentative connection with fantasy provides a field of potential whereby change can occur. The responses gathered will again shapeshift the questions as each drive is consciously explored and evaluated. If a substitution is made for the word "fantasy" with "innovation" or "vision" a concrete connection to corporate life may follow. To create an environment of innovation is to develop an environment where fantasy is welcomed. The most common aspect of any culture is a shared language and a shared view of reality, or a common way of thinking. To move an organization away from the bottom-line language of profitability towards a language of fantasy demands a powerful force. Current research on highly successful organizations is helping this shift in perspective take place. For when profitability can be directly linked to the dynamics of a corporate culture, managers start to pay attention. Deal and Kennedy agree and state:

> We find another point of similarity between visionary and culturally robust companies when we look at the relative importance of a shared set of core values compared to a narrow set of immediate objectives such as profit maximization.[8]

Initiation can be used to demarcate the boundary between the traditional industrial mode of thinking and the new knowledge-based paradigm. Using an archetypal approach to designing a rite of initiation becomes useful in that an archetypal focus permits, if not encourages, a tension of the opposites. Holding both the core values of the past along with the flexibility to respond to changing marketing forces can be contained in an archetypal vessel. A balance can be maintained between tradition, which provides a psychological anchor of safety, and innovation, the generative act that moves either the individual or the organization forward. Holding the tension of the opposites provides a psychological move toward a both/and position rather than the limiting stance of either/or. Deal and Kennedy, in *The New Corporate Cultures,* explore the balance between management actions needed to stay competition and the needs of workers to engage in meaningful activity:

> Good companies go to great efforts to make sure that new arrivals learn their historical roots. They understand that it is from history that the symbolic glue congeals to hold a group of people together and bond them to their shared mythology and enabling purpose.[9]

Deal and Kennedy believe that a "shared narrative of the past lays the foundation for culture"[10] and they caution against the loss of these historical roots in favor of whatever is currently in vogue. Again, the emphasis is on a shared mythology that honors the past and holds a common purpose for the future. To hold fast to this core provides an anchor that enables the organization to respond to changing market forces yet remain true to its roots.

Acts of initiation can communicate otherwise intangible beliefs and values. What an organization chooses to celebrate directly communicates what that organization values and thus becomes an important tool in examining a corporate culture. Daily work rituals also carry this tacit information and much, much more:

> But work rituals have a deeper symbolic meaning as well. Just below the surface, they are physical enactments of important values. In acting out a ritual, we reinforce intangibles that are difficult to convey in spoken language. In ritual, behavior speaks and helps us feel and connect with things below the conscious level. It helps groups to prepare themselves for cultural duties.[11]

Organizations are human institutions, not five-year plans, strategic analysis, or the ever-present, over-used bottom line. When conscious awareness of this fact is heightened, then organizational change must begin with the people that reside within the organization. Archetypal psychology allows a broader perspective in that both extremes of such consciousness are always available. Therefore, a conscious act of choice by the individual will either support or destroy efforts to change.

Every organization develops ways of identifying membership in the organization. To re-vision initiation as a generative force, requires that one examine the initiation rituals already in place. If an individual or an organization has spent enough time and reflection on aspects of the Call, (what it is that is hungered for), then a purpose, albeit rudimentary has been established.

The next stage of this journey asks for a boundary place that demarcates two states of being, to recognize that an act of beginning has been made. In the last chapter, it was noted that the participants created a Touchstone, an artistic act that denoted membership in their particular tribe. Any newcomer to the group would be asked, as a rite of passage, to contribute to the Touchstone created by the original group. Both individual and group boundaries were already established in this case. To use a symbolic or metaphorical technique to cross this boundary can be accomplished by using a rite of passage, an act of initiation.

Initiation and Recognition

Any organization that has cultivated its identity by making heroes, identifying its values and beliefs, creating rites and rituals and continually reinforcing this identity in its corporate culture will have a competitive edge. For such an organization provides meaning to its workforce, a common goal that binds its employees in a shared vision. This does not say that the organization will have a positive impact on society. Enron also had a strong corporate culture. So did Nazi Germany. The research would seem to indicate that it doesn't matter what the core value system entails. What matters is that one is in place. Choice plays an important role in whether the core value system will be seen as a positive or negative force by the employee and by the community in which the organization resides. What management rewards determines the actions of the workforce. Thus, the importance and the value of recognition in supporting behaviors management wishes to encourage.

As a manager, recognition would first be utilized in choosing the right people. Jim Collins, in *Good to Great,* presents a working hypothesis that great companies are made by choosing great people. In his description of what he terms "Level 5 Leaders," the parallels between the process of individuation and his "Level 5 Leadership" are clear:

> My hypothesis is that there are two categories of people: those who do not have the seed of Level 5 and those who do. The first category consists of people who could never in a million years bring themselves to subjugate their egoistic needs to the great ambition of building something larger and more lasting than themselves. For these people, work will always be first and foremost about what they *get*—fame, fortune, adulation, power, whatever—not what they *build*, create, and contribute. The second category of people—and I suspect the larger group—consists of those who have the potential to evolve to

Level 5; the capability resides within them, perhaps buried or ignored, but there nonetheless. And under the right circumstances—self-reflection, conscious personal development, a mentor, a great teacher, loving parents, a significant life experience, a Level 5 boss, or any number of other factors—they begin to develop.[12]

To find individuals who are capable of working towards a higher goal than simply a paycheck is a difficult task. But Collins believes that if one finds those individuals and unites them around a common vision, then that group of individuals (or organization in a larger sense) is capable of responding to any market challenge with success. Such an emphasis on core beliefs, or in archetypal terms, a corporate mythology is a prerequisite for a company to make the transition from good to great. According to Collins, the characteristics of such an individual capable of becoming a Level 5 leader shown follows:

Characteristics of Level 5 Leadership[13]

Professional Will	Personal Humility
Creates superb results, a clear catalyst in the transition from good to great.	Demonstrates a compelling modesty, shunning public adulation; never boastful.
Demonstrates an unwavering resolve to do whatever must be done to produce the best long-term results, no matter how difficult.	Acts with quiet, calm determination; relies principally on inspired standards, not inspiring charisma, to motivate.
Sets the standard of building an enduring great company; will settle for nothing less.	Channels ambition into the company, not the self; sets up successors for even greater success in the next generation.
Looks in the mirror, not out the window, to apportion responsibility for poor results, never blaming other people, external factors, or bad luck.	Looks out the window, not in the mirror, to apportion credit for the success of the company—to other people, external factors, and good luck.

To make a move away from purely ego-driven need to recognition that one is a part of a larger whole, mimics the process of individuation where the ego must acknowledge, if not bow to, the desires of the Self. As Collins describes it, that call to Level 5 Leadership can be instigated by a number of factors, again mimicking the process of individuation. For under the right circumstances the egoic demands may be ignored in favor of a greater good. Perhaps this is a lofty statement, and certainly one that is problematic, but to expand a life through recognition, relationship and meaning is the goal of individuation and seems to play an importance role in corporate success as well.

Recognition also contributes to the process of an individual seeking a corporate environment that matches a personal value system. If the organization maintains and actively promotes its corporate culture, such promotion becomes a visible beacon for potential employees. How such communication of corporate culture can be accomplished and maintained will be reviewed more extensively in the next chapter.

Initiation and Relationship

As previously noted, initiation symbolizes the beginning of something new which also implies an ending. The rites of passage that accomplish initiation as a function of relationship are important in establishing corporate culture. How an organization accepts a new member demonstrates both espoused values and values-in-action. How well the relationship between individual and manager develops will depend on the consistency of relationship between espoused values and value-in-action. Core values exhibited in day-to-day operations will serve as guides in making choices in behavior. In *The New Corporate Cultures,* Deal and Kennedy emphasize this aspect of a living example:

> Strong company cultures arise because of leadership displayed by senior managers at some point in the past. Such leadership has little to do with charisma. It has a lot to do with serving as a visible, living example of core values that become central to the culture.[14]

If the organization has a strong "identity" lived by its leaders, then any new employee has a better understanding of what is expected on a day-to-day basis. If the culture of the organization is clearly defined by what standards are to be maintained and by what means, the new employee is much more likely to make decisions that support those standards. The ways in which new employees are welcomed also carry tacit information about the organization itself. For example, in the profession of law, a new lawyer is "called to the Bar" (in Canada, the Bar meaning the Bar Association of the province in which the new initiate resides). A ceremony at the provincial law courts is held with all provincial judges in attendance, the families of the new lawyers and representatives of the law firms in that jurisdiction. The judges wear the ceremonial robes of the court. The new initiates into the practice of law are "called" to present themselves before the judges, accompanied by the mentors assigned to each student. The new lawyer swears an oath that he or she will abide by the professional code of ethics. They are welcomed to the practice of law by each judge individually while those assembled act as witnesses to the oath. The relationship between the young initiate and the established practitioners is clearly defined. The standards of performance and code of conduct is set. The ritual establishes a demarcation. After the ceremony, the initiate is now a member of an elite force that represents justice to each other, the community of the Bar, and the society that the Bar serves. There is no return and individual responsibility to Self, the Bar community and society is now forever changed. This initiation, a rite of passage, has been enacted for hundreds of years. A new relationship has been forged and is intended to last a lifetime. After the "Call to the Bar" has been completed, each new lawyer, no longer a law student, returns to the law firm that sponsored the individual at which another ceremony takes place to welcome the new lawyer into the practice of law. All members of the law firm attend such events and celebrate the successful passage from student to practitioner. It is an experience no lawyer forgets. As it is intended.

Initiation and Meaning

Perhaps in no other aspect of organizational life is the act of initiation more needed. In making a shift from an industrial paradigm to a knowledge paradigm, rites of passage provide structure in organizational culture. Again, the importance of a guide or mentor is invaluable in navigating the tacit aspects of corporate culture. More than just verbal guidance, the wisdom imparted by the mentor to the initiate enables the new member of the organization to assimilate both the explicit and tacit rules and regulations of corporate life. As Jung remarks: "The mere use of words is futile if you do not know what they stand for."[15] The impartation of meaning can make or break a corporate career, particularly in a global economy where communication is particularly important. To help learn the language of the environment, and to teach any hidden meanings associated with that language, is a function of the mentor or guide. Shared or core values delineate the purpose of the organization and the role of the mentor or ally is to elaborate on the core value so that any hidden meaning becomes available to the initiate. Core values can provide the cohesive strength that binds the people in an organization together in service of a common goal. Some examples are found as follows:

Examples of Core Values and their Meaning[16]

Value Statement	Meaning
Caterpillar: "24-hour parts service anywhere in the world"	symbolizes an extraordinary commitment to meeting customer needs
Leo Burnett Advertising Agency: "Make great ads"	Commitment to a particular concept of excellence
American Telephone & Telegraph: "Universal service"	A historical orientation towards standardized, highly reliable service to all possible users, now being reshaped into values more relevant to a newly competitive marketplace
DuPont: "Better things for better living through chemistry"	A belief that product innovation, arising out of chemical engineering, is DuPont's most distinctive value
Sears, Roebuck: "Quality at a good price"	The mass merchandiser for middle America.
Rouse Company: "Create the best environment for people"	A dominating concern to develop healthy and pleasant residential communities, not just to build subdivisions.
Continental Bank: "We'll find a way"	To meet customer needs
Dana Corporation: "Productivity through People"	Enlisting the ideas and commitment of employees at every level in support of Dana's strategy of competing largely on cost and dependability rather than product differentiation
Chubb Insurance Company: "Underwriting excellence"	An overriding commitment to excellence in a critical function
Price Waterhouse & Company: "Strive for technical perfection"	In accounting

The success of each organization listed above is dependent upon how well the espoused values translate into values-in-action, or core values. For each individual drawn to the organization because of the espoused values, retention of that individual will also be a factor of how well the value system translates into daily activity. To work from an archetypal perspective incorporates the values and beliefs of the individual and the values and beliefs of the organization. The purpose of the Heroic Journey as a visual aid allows the development of a link between the individual and the organization through the multiple qualities of recognition, relationship, and meaning. As such, archetypal psychology is well suited for this task, as Jung explains:

> Psychology is the only science that has to take the factor of value (feeling) into account, since it forms the link between psychic events on the one hand, and meaning and life on the other.[17]

To build initiation rites that serve to introduce an individual to a specific way of being in the world or a specific value system enables the individual to participate more fully in organizational life. In other words, the interior value system of the individual can be linked to an external source such as an organization through aspects of recognition, relationship and meaning.

So How Does It Work?

Part of the choice of change is that the process can be a bit chaotic. It is easy to fall back into old habits, simply because they are familiar. As a leader, part of the challenge is to balance the new with the old. Envision Financial CEO, Gord Huston comments:

> Initiation of ideas and thought leadership is challenging for organizations particularity those organizations that are so heavily structured and rules based, like financial institutions. When Envision was created, one of the things we identified that we had to be successful, is champions of change. We decided to make it a strategic objective to create a spirit within the organization of innovation and to measure our progress in the eyes of the staff and of our member-owners each year. This step helped create the freedom for people in the organization to be thought leaders and think originally. But lest I paint too rosy a picture, on our worst day we fall back into old habits, but I am pleased to say that on our best day we nurture new ideas, supports conceptual thinking and invite people to express their view. Naturally, we continually have to remind ourselves to support and protect ideas in their initial stages. One of the hardest things in this area is to say no, but encourage the thought leader to keep those channels open.

A way to keep those channels open is the identification of potential leaders within the organization. Such identification can be onerous. It requires planning, something that most organizations do badly, being reactive rather than proactive. Again, to shift to a proactive stance, and re-vitalize the skill of long term planning, allows for growth from within. Research indicates that growing your own leaders is much more successful in the long-term than importing new leaders from outside the organization.

If generativity can be expressed within ongoing leadership and succession planning within an organization, what does such generativity look like in practical terms? Again, I return to Envision Financial.

The educational programs devised followed standard university courses with the exception that class assignments could also be focused towards the development of the credit union itself. A head office was constructed that also housed the corporate university, allowing employees easy access to continuing education. Courses were offered during the workday in order not to disturb family time, an important corporate value.

As the number of graduates increased, their value to the organization increased. The credit union develops its management internally, decreasing employee turnover and absenteeism and increasing employee satisfaction. Establishing a demarcation point in education, the credit union established a core value for the institution and established a rite of passage for its new leadership, grown from within. The organization established a strong connection between espoused values and values-in-action.

Profitability continued to increase, which increased shareholder value. The program is such an obvious success that the executive and the board of directors of the credit union decided to consider the development of an MBA program to increase both the potential of each individual employee and profitability to the organization itself. Advice from degree-granting institutions was sought and again, a program is being put in place that supports both short and long-term goals of the credit union.

To calculate return on investment (ROI) in this instance would be impossible. The transformation from uneducated to professional status not only has a positive effect upon the internal culture of this organization but also continues to make an invaluable contribution to individual, family, and community. The lives of all members of the family have been affected. The long-term influence upon the children of these employees has yet to be measured, if indeed such measurement is even possible. Certainly from a qualitative stance, the ramifications are profound. Several archetypes of transformation were considered in the decision to make this educational program possible, as Jung's words imply:

> If the flow of instinctive dynamism into our life is to be maintained, as is absolutely necessary for our existence, then it is imperative that we should remould

these archetypal forms into ideas which are adequate to the challenge of the present.[18]

To meet current organizational needs, several aspects were emphasized. First is the recognition that formal education provides a form of financial independence, particularly important to single women with children. To use safety as a primordial archetype of transformation, the organization was able to transform such a primary need into tangible reality. Second, the organization confirmed its commitment to the concept of family, both individually and collectively, thus living its brand. The individual family unit was strengthened, with potential for enhancing the value of education passed from adult to child. It is one thing to state the importance of education; it is quite another to participate in living the experience of having a parent attend school at the same time as the affected child. The espoused value becomes a value-in-action, a lived experience as well as a theoretical concept. The collective unit of the credit union was also influenced as all members, whether participating in the program or not, witnessed the efforts of both individual and organization alike to make this program a living reality.

As a form of initiation, the program re-visioned the credit union's understanding of leadership. Creating from within instead of seeking leadership from without defines the organization's commitment to recognition of talent within its ranks. All employees are aware of this program and each individual decides whether to pursue such a vibrant option. The organization then demonstrates its dedication to individual choice by providing an option not available without the organization's assistance.

Thus, this credit union not only generates its own committed leadership from within the organizational ranks, but also ensures succession of the core values and beliefs of the organization itself. The long-term effect on client retention has yet to be determined. However, the organization's reputation in the community has been positive and continues to expand as more community members become aware of the efforts of the organization. The community supports the decision of the credit union by increasing its membership in the organization itself. As the organization expands through the growth of new members, more funds become available to create educational programs. From this actual growth the funds for the MBA program originate.

The core value system of the institution and the core value system of the individuals within it have been linked, in this particular case, by the core value of generative leadership. Both have benefited from such an approach. Organizational needs have been served by aiding the employees who participate in their journey to individuation.

An exploration of this journey of individuation will be explored in more detail in the next chapter.

Notes—Initiation:

1. Barnhart, 388.

2. Jung, CW8: 107.

3. Joel Bakan, The Corporation, 6. This is a book that will either delight you or horrify you or even, both. Bakan explores organizational behaviour in a harsh light. Either way, the book or the movie will expand your awareness of corporate behaviour and its potential destructive aspects.

4. Buckingham and Coffman, 257.

5. Ibid, 256.

6. Jung, CW9i: 80

7. Hillman, Re-Visioning Psychology, 23.

8. Deal and Kennedy, Corporate Cultures, 27.

9. Deal and Kennedy, The New Corporate Cultures, 4.

10. Ibid, 4.

11. Ibid, 6.

12. Collins, Good to Great, 36.

13. Ibid.

14. Deal and Kennedy, The New Corporate Cultures, 30.

15. Jung, The Undiscovered Self, 137.

16. Deal and Kennedy, Corporate Cultures, 23.

17. Jung, The Undiscovered Self, 140.

18. Ibid, 39.

The Ordeal—Activity

How and why people do the work they do, can be expressed in the third drive, that of activity. The description of the work performed is influenced by its contextuality, the workplace as a society. When one views organizations through the lens of culture, one sees mini-societies with distinctive values, rituals, and ideologies. To place the work performed in an organization within the metaphor of the Heroic Journey, using the term *Ordeal* in the context of organizational life may be appropriate. In *Values Shift,* authors Izzo and Withers comment on our current demographic shift to less available employees:

> Given that by 2006, half of all workers will be employed in information technology positions or within industries that intensively utilize information technology, products and services, this shortfall presents a crisis. [1]

Cultural norms within an organization are changing, necessitating a shift in the transfer of economic power from an industrial to a knowledge model. The difficulty of this shift in perspective should not be underestimated.

In addition, as demographics shift to accommodate a smaller number of individuals in the workforce, the way in which work is allocated and performed in any organization needs to be re-visioned. Organizations will need the same amount or more work done, and fewer and fewer individuals will be available to complete the required tasks.

Current corporate cultures are built around the old industrial model evidenced by distinct concepts of work and leisure, and routines of work that are based on working from Monday to Friday, scheduled from nine to five each day. With a move towards a knowledge economy, such constraints need to be removed in order to allow both individuals and organizations more flexibility in response to a changing global environment and shifting demographics.

In my work with organizations, recognition of this shift in perspective is only superficially acknowledged, which results in a demoralized workforce that is compelled to work harder in order to compensate for staff shortages. In Human Resource terminology, "thinking outside the box" is a popular expression used in an attempt to move away from a command/control environment. The problem with such a demand is that current knowledge workers are already "outside the box." The organization and its leaders are now the prisoners in a paradigm that no longer works. Today's knowledge workers are demanding something more than just a job or paycheck from an organization. If basic drives such as hunger and sexuality, or generativity as it is used in this context, are satisfied, then the drive to activity will begin to emerge. Jung elaborates further:

> I should like, then, to differentiate as a third group of instincts the *drive to activity*. This urge starts functioning when the other urges are satisfied; indeed, it is perhaps only called into being after this has occurred. Under this heading would come the urge to travel, love of change, restlessness, and the play-instinct.[2]

After the first two drives have been appeased, an individual may begin to focus on the type of work performed and the relationship with others in the workplace. As an instinct, the drive to activity also includes what Jung terms "love of change." Such a belief needs incorporation into an organization's corporate mythology. The current emphasis on hierarchical job descriptions and standardized methods of performing tasks must shift toward the talents and strengths an individual may bring to the organization. By so doing, the organization provides a field of potential for each employee dependent upon individual talent rather than a fixed job description or career position. Deal and Kennedy maintain that superior performance by an organization is dependent upon the culture of the organization and as such, will drive future profitability.

> The culture of an organization is the interwoven, organic system of beliefs, values, rituals, personalities, characters, and mythology that creates meaning for people at work. When it hangs together, culture produces extraordinary loyalty among the members and often extraordinary efforts in pursuit of shared goals. This in turn produces superior performance over the long term. It is vital to financial success.[3]

To understand a corporate culture requires a deepened examination in order to expose what creates meaning for people at work. The deeper level may or may not be consistent with the espoused values of the organization. Indeed, when a disconnect occurs within an individual between the deeper internal levels of thought and perception and external overt behavior, we call such a condition a neurosis. An organization can suffer from the same condition. Jung was fond of pointing out "when the intellect does not serve the symbolic life it is the devil; it makes you neurotic."[4] In some organizations, corporate life suffers from being too one-sided, over-emphasizing an egoic, short-term thinking which makes no room for intuitive expression through the feeling function. To rectify this condition, whether in an individual or an organization, a move towards clarifying both espoused values and values-in-action is required.

I know of no greater resource in an organizational setting than the art of story and collecting stories; through story an individual or an organization communicates Jung's drive of activity. "Story" shares a common etymology with "history." Both words derive from Latin, *historia*, meaning "account" or "tale" and the Greek *historiā*, meaning "record" or "inquiry."[5] In the Heroic Journey model, the deepest part of the image contains the "Ordeal," which meaning originates from Old English about 1365, in *ordal*—"a method of trial by physical test."[6] The story told communicates meaning; the telling describes what the teller values and as such, may provide a panoptic view. It is a powerful aid that can be used to elicit tacit meaning. Story lives in the realm of poesis, meaning combining forms, or indicating the act of making or producing something (from Greek *poiêsis*). Storytelling is a poetic activity. The storyteller transforms an event into an experience that then can be shared between the teller and the listener. In other words, telling a story involves the transformation of everyday events into meaningful experience. Aristotle believed that poetry was superior to history, as poetry tends to explore possibilities as well as what has actually taken place. In the *Poetics,* he states:

> The distinction is this: the one says what has happened, the other the kind of thing that would happen. For this reason poetry is more philosophical and more serious than history. Poetry tends to express universals, and history particulars. The *universal* is the kind of speech or action which is consonant with a person of a given kind in accordance with probability or necessity; this is what poetry aims at, even though it applies individual names. [...] So it is clear from these points that the poet must be a maker of plots rather than of verses, insofar as he is a poet with respect to imitation, and the object of his imitation is action.[7]

In the case of an organization, the stories told become the institutionalized memory of the organization itself and carry the "universal truth" of the organization. Most tales told in organizational settings communicate aspects of "the Ordeal" or testing stage of the Heroic Journey. Tales of the Ordeal describe difficulties that were encountered and then overcome or alternatively, the difficulties that could not be defeated. The Hero/ines within the organization all become part of the memory of the organization and the tales surrounding them become stories that act as a form of myth-making or poesis. For a new member, these stories represent what can be done, what should be done, and what may be done. For an established member of the organization, these stories are a way of communicating that individual's status within the "tribe," establishing his or her place in the organization.

Stories carry tremendous power. Even if the information is historically inaccurate, it would still have an impact that dry facts cannot. In *The Story Factor*, Annette Simmons addresses this power:

> Story is indirect, when directness won't work. Other forms of influence like reward, bargaining, bribery, rhetoric, coercion, and trickery are too tightly focused on the desired outcome. These tactics actually stimulate resistance because they don't give people enough elbow room. Story is a more dynamic tool of influence. Story gives people enough space to think for themselves. A story develops and grows in the mind of your listener. [8]

As with any communication tool, this is a power that can be used for either productive or destructive ends. It all depends on the message and the intent of the teller. In *Corporate Legends & Lore*, consultant Peg C. Neuhauser addresses the shadow side of storytelling in organizations:

> A cynical approach to a story usually makes it very clear that the listener should not hope for any improvements in the future. In other words, they are not just condemning the past behaviors and practices in the organization. They are also writing off the future as hopeless. There is often a large element of "victim" mindset in cynical storytellers. They see themselves as having been harmed in the past and powerless to stop this sort of thing from happening again in the future. "Victims" thinkers are usually angry and frightened, and that is what they communicate in their stories. [9]

Neuhauser has conducted extensive research on the negative aspects of storytelling and terms it the *90 Percent Factor*. She explains:

> Over one hundred audiences of managers and employees from different companies were asked to think of a story that they had heard or told in the past few weeks about their organization. When asked to vote on whether the story they had in mind was positive, negative or neutral in the message that it carried about the company, *over 90 percent of every audience voted negative.*

If this informal survey of storytelling in organizations is an accurate reflection of what is really going on out there in companies, this is a very dangerous situation. Any culture that tells over 90 percent negative stories to itself about itself is being destroyed from the inside out. [10]

The stories told also represent a difference between information handling and story-telling. Information handling is those bits of factual data needed to conduct the affairs of the organization, the particulars of any job function. Storytelling carries meaning. To use the Heroic Journey as a visual map can aid the telling of tales in organizational life and can rescue meaning that may otherwise become buried in a constant supply of information. To pay close attention to the stories told will allow a determination as to the potential positive or negative effect on both individual and corporate culture.

Archetypal branding expert, Edward Wachtman, in describing the function of an evaluator in an organization, emphasizes the narrative aspect of corporate storytelling:

[T]he evaluator is engaged in creating a story from the first moments of the evaluation effort, that the emphasizing of particular facts and events represents a fundamental structuring of information that is basic to storytelling. This structure is narrative. [11]

Narratives involve the narrator's active engagement with the story. The response invited by the story is to engage with its meaning. Or, in other words, the function of narrative is the art of using words to produce pictures in the mind of the listener. Those pictures combine with the situation at hand to create a powerful lasting message capable of producing change. If the peripety or change in circumstance is strong enough in the aspects of the Ordeal, two emotions will tend to emerge: empathy, which refers to the listener's identification with the story; and fear, wherein the listener is relieved that the circumstances did not happen to him or her. It is much easier to hear the circumstances surrounding another's test of courage than to participate in one's own test. In the same vein, the story may also invite action by the listener; even providing the courage for the listener to progress in her or his life. According to Peg Neuhauser, "without storytelling, any culture—whether it is a traditional tribe or a large corporation—would have a very difficult time protecting and passing on the best of its culture."[12] Storytelling in organizations is analogous to poetic work; both seek to transcend the literal event and offer a deeper, more powerful, meaningful experience. Wachtman believes that:

> It is an underlying force that shapes the way we perceive our lives, the lives of others, our past, our present, and the possibility of our future. Narrative is the fundamental framework on which our histories and fictions are built and our stories told, and upon which evaluation activities must also rest. It is narrative that eliminates the apparent contradictions between history and fiction and which enables us to look at the possibility of comparing evaluating and storytelling.[13]

Telling a story demonstrates to the listener who one is and what one values, and as such, storytelling can be used as an evaluative function in examining and exploring a corporate culture. The listener receives detailed information about the teller and the setting of the story itself, the organization. Storytelling can demonstrate the complexity of organizational life since stories are polysemic, that is evoking different or even conflicting meanings. The story may resonate in diverse or contradictory ways within a single individual. According to Peg Neuhauser, "Stories allow a person to feel and see the information as well as factually understand it."[14]

Therein lies the importance of the Heroic Journey as a container for the story. The map itself can be a symbolic representation of coping with the emotional aspects of change; it provides a framework for the narrative and indicates both a particular point in time and the visual representation of the continuation of time. Wachtman concurs, and suggests that

> [n]arrative and time are intimately bound together, because it is by structuring the experience of our actions in time—by the stories that we tell about ourselves (and to ourselves) and about others—that we are able to create a sense of unity and wholeness from the innumerable, discrete events that make up our individual and collective lives. To exist temporally is to exist narratively; it is to have a story.[15]

Particular aspects of the Ordeal can be expressed by looking at the aspects of recognition, relationship, and meaning. How an individual responds to being tested throughout the Ordeal is the stuff of individuation. The stories told demonstrate the emotional character held by the teller, what is behavior is valued, and what is rejected. In collecting the narratives of the individual in an organization, one can obtain an overview of the corporate culture. In order to predict future performance, the Gallup Organization has developed a statistical representation.

I have found that using both, the collection and analysis of stories and statistical analysis, offers an accurate reading of a particular corporate culture as well as an accurate evaluation of individual development. Both are necessary.

Ordeal and Recognition

When the Gallup organization compiled the research results from its questionnaire, the Q12, the results and the questions were broken down into four separate categories. The first, Base Camp or "What do I get," was described as the starting place of a new role. At this level, needs are fairly basic. A new employee would want to know the location of various services such as washrooms, kitchen facilities, locker rooms, his or her desk or working location, basic salary and benefits, to name a few. Of the twelve questions, these two measure Base Camp needs:

1. Do I know what is expected of me at work?

2. Do I have the materials and equipment I need to do my work right?[16]

These questions could be used as an analogy for the initial drive of hunger fulfilling basic emotional needs. For each new role within an organization, the individual would return to the most basic of psychological requirements. Having these fundamentals in place allows the individual to begin to expand his or her understanding of the role undertaken.

The next series of questions addresses individual contribution and the perception held by others, whether management or co-workers, of the individual's contribution to the organization. Gallup termed this stage Camp 1 or "What do I give?" and is represented by the following questions:

3. At work, do I have the opportunity to do what I do best every day?

4. In the last seven days, have I received recognition or praise for doing good work?

5. Does my supervisor, or someone at work, seem to care about me as a person?

6. Is there someone at work who encourages my development?[17]

To address these questions requires a shift from thinking about only the immediate needs of the self to the self in relationship to others which is the beginning of the individuation process.

Each of these questions helps you know not only if you feel you are doing well in the role (Q3), but also if other people value *your individual performance* (Q4), if they value *you as a person* (Q5), and if they are prepared to *invest in your growth* (Q6). These questions all address the issue of your *individual* self-esteem and worth. As we will see, if these questions remain unanswered, all of your yearnings to belong, to become part of a team, to learn and to innovate, will be undermined.[18]

Ordeal and Relationship

The third series of the Gallup Q12 questions addresses the concern of "Do I belong here?" and is represented by the following questions:

7. At work, do my opinions seem to count?

8. Does the mission/purpose of my company make me feel my job is important?

9. Are my co-workers commited to doing quality work?

10. Do I have a best friend at work?[19]

Whatever the specific value orientation of the individual, at this stage the question is whether the worker feels that there exists a "fit" between him or her and the organization. Such a "fit" can also be located in the types of stories told by the worker that represent the interplay between management and the employee. As such, the stories also become a way of "knowing'" the corporate culture. Wachtman suggests that

> [n]arrative is a way of knowing because through it we isolate particular events, describe them in a particular manner, and place them into structured and ordered relationships with one another. Through narrative we make comprehensible the countless interrelationships that comprise our lives. These interrelationships form the unified patterns, themes, and motifs that tie independent actions and events together in a sequence that we call a story.[20]

If indeed management believes that its employees cannot be trusted, the corporate culture will indicate such lack of trust in the stories told within the organization. Through such a collected narrative, an examination can be made of the interrelationships between management and employee that can be compared to a statistical evaluation such as the Q12. Such a combined approach will provide ample material by which to diagnose the corporate culture.

Ordeal and Meaning

In the last portion of the Q12, the questions address what the Gallup organization terms "The Summit." When all the other questions or needs have been addressed, these questions will come into play:

11. In the last six months, has someone at work talked to me about my progress?

12. This last year, have I had opportunities at work to learn and grow?[21]

Both of these questions address how the individual feels about the relationship with the organization and how the organization responds to the individual. Emphasis is still placed on individual development within the organizational setting. As such, the course of individuation can be tracked in a statistical framework that provides a correlation to corporate profitability, productivity, employee retention, and customer satisfaction. This type of analysis also shows whether individuation could occur in a corporate setting. If the scores indicate a strong foundation, as reported by the individuals within the organization, then a basic level of trust and safety could be assumed to exist in the interplay between management and employees. I would suspect that individuation is more likely in such an organization but more research needs to be conducted before any conclusive statement could be made. Wachtman suggest that

> through narrative, stories structure our perception of our experience in life so that we are secure in our past, alive in our present, and hopeful for a future. [...] They help us give coherent meaning to the multitude of events and objects that pass through, and intersect with, our daily lives by offering an internal logic on which to construct sequential relationships.[22]

James Hillman believes that by staying with the process of individuation within the organization is the way to making the required paradigm shift. He advises that ""pathologizing the myth onward" means staying in the mess while at the same time regarding what is going on from a mythical perspective."[23]. An archetypal perspective to corporate culture allows the tension of the opposites to be maintained until the transcendent function begins to operate. Due to the psychological tension of conflicting ideas, the "Ordeal" is aptly named. But such a deepening of psychological experience allows a space for both innovation and tradition to flourish.

Analysis of the stories told within an organization reflects aspects of recognition, relationship, and meaning and therefore provide an overview of general corporate health which may be used to predict longevity. The value of using story as a diagnostic tool should not be underestimated, as story provides the psychological framework held by the individual and the psychological character valued by the organization. The difference between giving factual information or an example and telling a story is the addition of emotional content in the telling of the story. The story weaves details, people, and situations into a common values-in-action web. The use of story as a tool for transformation within an organization should become part of every manager's education. Policy and procedures tell people how to think. A story invites people to connect at an individual level to an organizational framework and places the control of how the story may continue back into the hands of the listener. The teller gives guidance through the telling of the story. The listener retains the power of how that story will be used to influence personal behavior.

So How Does It Work

To follow our story of Envision Financial, Gord Huston speaks to the challenges of transforming the organization:

> The organizational change to more openness to innovation such as EnvisonU continues to be a challenge. This is particularly true at budget time. New ideas often have no financial benefit to the organization in the year that they are initiated, in fact this might be true for several years forward. As the saying goes, "It's not good enough to think strategically, but stop thinking that way during budget time." This is where the CEO needs to get involved and express permission to create budgets around innovation as an investment in the future.

In terms of long-term strategy, Huston is fulfilling his obligations as a leader by thinking not only in immediate terms but also in terms of future potential and growth. The stated commitment by the executive is translated into action, including financial support for innovation. A long-term view is held while maintaining daily operational effectiveness. An open environment is created and maintained for individual potential to emerge.

Jung was fond of saying: "If the whole is to change, the individual must change himself."[24] If the opus, or the life's work of an individual, is what will serve the organization of the future, how does such an opus manifest in practical terms? A further example may illustrate the point.

A nonprofit organization was formed to address child rights and development. All members of the nonprofit organization had considerable experience in this field as well as in international relief work. All members of the executive team were highly educated and respected in their fields with considerable experience in both administration and field work. I was asked to design a program to enable the executive team to link their vision to existing international programs. One of the programs in particular seemed to capture the vision of this team.

Africa is currently struggling with an AIDS epidemic that is decimating the adult population. As a result, hundreds and possibly thousands of orphans exist now with no traditional family structure. To attempt to "parent" these large groups of children is an impossible task. Accordingly, an attempt is being made to "re-vision" the concept of parenting through establishing communities that serve as a parental structure and provide a safe haven or home. Part of the mandate of this agency was to provide support by education and training of AIDS workers who would attempt this task.

International relief work is demanding (both physically and psychologically). In the group's review and discussion of the core values that held the executive team together, it was discovered that the agency itself had no "home" that supported the team while individuals were in the field.

Home is a very powerful archetype that strikes at the core of any individual. For this group to re-vision home for others, it was also necessary for them to re-vision home for themselves. As the team worked with this image of a collective home and what it meant to them individually, the process enabled an expansion of the image itself. Jung offers the following insight: "A man whose heart is not changed will not change any other's."[25] It is one thing to grasp a difficult concept intellectually; it is another to grasp it with the heart. The following process may help distinguish the two.

Image played a very important role in envisioning a home base. A group of postcards were employed to provoke imaginal thinking. Each individual then spoke to the image and formed a story around the importance of "home." As the group underwent this process, it was decided that the current office space currently held did not have the necessary aspects of "home" that were uncovered using the images. A different location was found, negotiated, and obtained that allowed the team to shift its perspective.

Each team member brought to the new location a piece of art or other object that represented his or her individual interpretation of "home." A native elder was asked to attend a ceremony to welcome the new space and bless both the objects and the work to be undertaken by the team.

Working in this manner enabled the team to envision and more importantly, experience different ways of establishing a "home." First from an imaginal sense which then enables concretization of the image into a practical realization. The stories gathered and told around the meaning of "home" creates a bridge to shared understanding. The insights garnered by the executive team during this process are now being taught to members of the organization in the field. Their own experience has been deepened around the meaning of "home" and as such, will enhance their individual and collective ability to empathize with others. You can read about any concept, but in my view, nothing beats the power of lived experience. It is something that resonates within you at a deep level you never forget.

Notes—The Ordeal:

1. Izzo and Withers, Values Shift, 10. See also the work of Brian P. Hall, in his book of the same name published in 1994. The importance of values cannot be understated. Archetypes may be the territory with values being the map.

2. Jung, CW8: 240.

3. Deal and Kennedy, The New Corporate Cultures, 84.

4. Jung, CW18: 665.

5. Barnhart, 764.

6. Ibid, 526.

7. Aristole, The Poetics, 51b.

8. Annette Simmons, The Story Factor, 34. Simmons has produced a great book on the power of story within organizations. Full of entertaining examples, this book provides valuable tools for use in corporate storytelling.

9. Peg Neuhasuer, Corporate Legends & Lore, 7. Another excellent reference for the use of storytelling in organizations. This book examines the role of storytelling as a management tool and its capacity to strengthen the culture and spirit of the workplace.

10. Ibid, 9.

11. Wachtman, 90. Edward Wachtman is an expert in archetypal branding. Further information on his work and his organization can be found at http://www.storytellings.com

12. Neuhauser, 14.

13. Wachtman, 90.

14. Neuhauser, 5.

15. Wachtman, 93.

16. Buckingham and Coffman, 43.

17. Ibid, 44.

18. Ibid, 44.

19. Ibid.

20. Wachtman, 96.

21. Buckingham and Coffman, 45.

22. Wachtman, 97.

23. Hillman, Re-Visioning Psychology, 74.

24. Jung, CW18: 1378.

25. Jung, CW18: 1396.

•

Breakthrough—Reflection

The fourth aspect of the Heroic Journey is Breakthrough or in Jung's metamythology, Reflection. Archetypal psychology is a cultural movement that has its foundations in the imagination, the creative source in each individual. Anything that has been constructed by an individual existed first in the imagination as a dream, an idea, or even a partial thought. The imagination offers the capacity to ask "what if?" and it is from that point that innovation originates. It is with the acts of reflecting, thinking, dreaming, and fantasizing—that "what if" moments are translated from a potential to actual state. Jung states that "another instinct, different from the drive to activity and so far as we know specifically human, which might be called the *reflective instinct,*" is another aspect of our psyche that must be fulfilled.[1] Reflection, if we so choose, leads us to our creative source. The ability to imagine and re-member an experience is foundational to this phenomenological approach to organizational theory. Jung goes on to suggest:

> *Reflexio* is a turning inwards, with the result that, instead of an instinctive action, there ensues a succession of derivative contents or states which may be termed reflection or deliberation. Thus in place of the compulsive act there appears a certain degree of freedom, and in place of predictability a relative impredictability as to the effect of the impulse.[2]

This level of "impredictability" is a painful one. You must stay open to the possibilities that arise from reflections on the mythology of the corporation. To remain open to shifting ideas is difficult but necessary, for it allows a space for creative thought to birth a new approach, or idea.

Our ability to imagine provides the foundation for reflection, because remembering is an imaginal activity. Through such an activity, we are sometimes motivated to create something that gives form or expression to such remembering. Indeed, Jung felt that the creative impulse was strong enough to mediate between inner faith and outer knowledge and would cause neurosis if it was not healed through reflection.

The rupture between faith and knowledge is a symptom of the *split conscious-ness* which is so characteristic of the mental disorder of our day. It is as if two different persons were making statements about the same thing, each from his own point of view, or as if one person in two different frames of mind were sketching a picture of his experience. If for "person" we substitute "modern society", it is evident that the latter is suffering from a mental dissociation, i.e., a neurotic disturbance.[3]

The drive to reflection, to re-member or re-create experience, enables the creative act to take place. The use of the imaginal is self-evident, whether it may be used in the formulation of a marketing strategy, the development of training programs, or the construction of a corporate mythology. The ability to imagine can be considered the bedrock of innovation. Without the active imagination of some daring individual, there is no corporation to begin with. "All our inventions begin as ideas; all our material power derives from ideational power."[4] The Heroic Journey as a working model and a research methodology, allows for reflection that also includes an additional phase: to witness the multifaceted layers of meaning that arise. The potential for creativity is an archetypal force in its own right. What is needed is to bring back the language of the imaginal into the hallowed halls of business. James Hillman elaborates

[a]rchetypal thinking doesn't necessitate one-to-one equations, because this thinking is rooted in a polytheistic imagination in which the powers of ideas are interlinked and mutually influenced. There is no one sure truth, one sure identity, one sure explanation. The value of archetypal thinking is not so much to give sure identification to problems. Rather, it aims to open the mind to psychological reflection on the mind's stance and projects. [5]

In other words, to open the mind to transform an event into an experience, the ability to remember is needed and, more importantly, the ability to imagine. Phenomenologist Gaston Bachelard offers: "it is the imagination itself which thinks and which suffers."[6] The ability to imagine provides the foundation for reflection, for remembering is an imaginal activity. Through such activity we are sometimes motivated to create something that gives form or expression to such remembering.

In order to open the mind for psychological reflection, an individual cannot "think" his or her way through a creative process; the act of reverie or reflection will lead the individual to where the drive to creativity will express itself. To operate at this level of creativity is a form of soul making, which enables a psychological move to be made towards a language that can reach the soul of the corporation itself. Hillman reminds us:

> A new angelology of words is needed so that we may once again have faith in them. Without the inherence of the angel in the word—and angel means originally "emissary", "message-bearer"—how can we utter anything but personal opinions, things made up in our subjective minds? How can anything of worth and soul be conveyed from one psyche to another, as in a conversation, a letter, or a book, if archetypal significances are not carried in the depths of our words? [...] Words, like angels, are powers that have invisible power over us.[7]

There are some events in life that can only be articulated through analogy as the individual may not possess language that is sufficient to describe the event itself. Myths may be considered an expression of the way Psyche speaks analogically. Through a mythic approach, the psyche gains a voice by which to communicate archetypal significance.

Jung believes that the act of reflection was a necessary component of a human life and states "through the reflective instinct, the stimulus is more or less wholly transformed into a psychic content, that is, it becomes an experience: a natural process is transformed into a conscious content."[8]

When the imaginal emerges from a work, it may connect with individual memory, the ability to reflect on past experiences that are comparable to the work itself. It may also lead the individual to imagine places or situations that he or she had not thought possible. Bachelard believes that a "literary image can transport us from one universe to another."[9]

Through the richness of lived experience a life is defined. To adopt a mythic mode of being allows an individual to remain open to possibilities that have not been pursued nor even considered. Reflection enables possibility to become reality in order to transport us from one universe to another.

Breakthrough and Recognition

Bachelard writes: "By expressing itself in a new image, thought is enriched and enriches the language. Being becomes word. The word appears at the highest psychic point of being. The word reveals itself as the immediate mode of becoming of the human psyche."[10] The act of reflection seems to be a lost art, yet it is necessary to transform image into thought. In organizations today, time is a valuable commodity. Management initially resists the suggestion that reflection is a necessary component of the process of creative thinking.

By reflecting on the stories told within organizations, the story can become an element of organizational symbolism, an expression of perhaps unconscious desire or intent, or a vehicle for communication of possibilities. Focusing on a particular story or an aspect of a story, a *mythos*, is a way of making potential manifest into matter; giving the psyche form or soma. To use the Heroic Journey model as a vehicle for reflection can enable breakthrough thinking. To embody story in this form enables the individual to slightly disconnect from circumstance by placing the event contemplated into the third person form. As such, the story then can become once more a living thing; the individual has the possibility of changing the ending as previously perceived. James Hillman comments on this craft of exploration:

> We are not by nature psychological. Psychology must be gained for it is not given, and without psychological education we do not understand ourselves and we make our daimons suffer. This suggests that a reason for psychotherapy of whatever school and for whatever complaint is to gain psychology—a *logos* or soul that is at the same moment a *therapeia* of soul. We need to gain the intelligent response that makes the soul intelligible, a craft and order that understands it, a knowledgeable deftness that cares for its wants in speech. And if logos is its therapy, because it articulates the psyche's wants, then one answer to what the soul wants is psychology.[11]

The act of reflecting on the stories that are told can lead to a *therapeia* or healing of the circumstances surrounding the story. Storytelling in this sense becomes a tool, as Hillman claims, a "knowledgeable deftness" in manifesting a change.

Breakthrough and Relationship

The relationship between organizational stories and historical fact is complicated. It may seem simplistic to state that telling a story will reflect the perspective of the teller but a change in observation point can act as a catalyst for change in behavior. Organizational consultant Annette Simmons agrees and elaborates:

> Narration simultaneously chooses and communicates a particular point of view. When you want someone to "see" something they are obviously not seeing, then a story can take them on a tour of their choices/behaviors/inactivity from another perspective. Adding a new point of view to a listener's existing point of view expands what they see and can change how they think.[12]

Details of the story may be removed, change, or amplified in the telling, but the act of storytelling builds upon the potential for relationship between the teller and listener. What remains in an organizational story that is orally passed from person to person is the elemental pattern in the life of the organization that necessitates the telling. In this way, it is not the fact of the telling but the emotional message that is contained within the story that needs to be heard. Jungian Analyst Marie Louise von Franz further elaborates on this message:

> This shows that in fairy tales there is a pattern which fits into the unconscious of everybody and is therefore retained more securely. We know now that memory formation has to do with emotion. The more emotionally impressive something is, the more it sticks in the memory.[13]

Effective organizational stories carry an emotional level of meaning that stick in memory. Stories infuse historical events with meaning and, at times, compromise the accuracy of events. Consequently, it is also valuable to examine where the story has deviated from historical fact since the distortion may provide additional insight into the unconscious values held by the organization. One story may provide specific insight into an aspect of organizational life. In the collection of many organizational stories however, a pattern begins to reveal itself which defines the relationship between the organization and the individuals who comprise it. Thus, the core value system that permeates the organization can be exposed. Von Franz suggests:

> But if we put many stories together, we see that each one enlightens some typical archetypal process in the collective unconscious. If you put two or three hundred together, then you get a kind of intuitive mapping of the structure of the collective unconscious and the possible structures and processes in it.[14]

Such an intuitive mapping can be located at a particular place on the visual representation of the Heroic Journey. The role of the archetypal psychologist is to welcome this process and encourage reflection on what stories are presented in the role of a fellow-traveler on the journey itself. To encourage the telling allows the teller freedom of expression through the use of reverie and active imagination without confining the telling only to the discourse of facts. The findings of Annette Simmons speak to this freedom of expression:

> A subtle yet powerful shift occurs when you seek to influence people to make wise decisions rather than "right" decisions. When you decide to awaken

sleeping wisdom rather than to convince others you are right, you will produce a much more powerful experience for both of you. If you trust that the
wisdom is in the room, then your only job is to free this wisdom to flow
among the people.[15]

To encourage this flow, you need to be cautious in that the stories remain in a
natural state and are not presented for the benefit of an outsider. Judgment of the
stories presented should be avoided. Building trust is absolutely necessary in this
type of approach and the researcher needs to empathize with the vulnerability of
the teller. If an appropriate *temenos* can be constructed and then maintained by
the mythologist, the collective unconscious or wisdom can be accessed in the
interplay between the tension of the opposites, logical thought, and emotional
image, both of which are present in the telling of story. Von Franz explains:

> There are two compensatory realms in the collective. Both are deficient, and
> only when they unite is balance restored. To put it in general terms, the basic
> story line is to bring together two separate realms within the collective area of
> feeling and thinking.[16]

As fellow-travelers on the journey, we can, without judgment, encourage the
interplay between aspects of feeling and thinking surrounding the story itself and
reflection upon it. Questions should be asked in the spirit of continuing the dialogue between the tension of the opposites and should elicit additional interest
and pleasure in the process. Simmons believes that "facts are neutral until human
beings add their own meaning to those facts."[17] During a reflective process, one
might pose the following question: "What resonates within you to the story?"
The ability to speak of what is moving within an individual in a group setting
allows further reflection and expansion of the power of the story itself. A circumambulation of the process mirrors the behavior I wish to elicit from participants
in the process; as such, dreaming the dream onward may evoke new psychic
material that can break into conscious awareness. As Simmons succinctly states,
"People don't need new facts—they need a new *story*"[18]

Breakthrough and Meaning

In reflecting upon the work fantasized and then performed, the challenge is to
translate such creative formulation into the language of the corporation without
reducing its emotional meaning. Passion is a force that needs to be handled creatively. In a depth psychological approach, this necessitates an uroboric deepening of the evaluation process of creativity itself. This uroboric deepening, or

circling the layers of meaning, accesses unspoken constructs that form the organization. In James Hillman's words, "Deepening insists: no avoidance and no escape. Stay planted. No leave of absence. Clean up the mess."[19]

To satisfy the drive of reflection and to accomplish a breakthrough on the Heroic Journey, we reach a crossroads and the culmination of the initial study of the organization. Make no mistake, in order to evaluate accurately the corporate mythology that is functioning within an organization takes time and patience. It would be easy to stay in the superficial realm of marketing gimmicks, but such a practice does not touch the force that drives a successful marketing campaign. Instead, an archetypal or depth approach offers a container that will hold the complexity and the multiplicity of belief systems in an organizational structure, until a synthesized mythology can be recognized and then given language. The building of such a container is a function of management. Schein believes:

> From a cultural perspective, then, the essence of the leader's job is not how to create an organizational culture but how to manage the diversity of subcultural forces that are already operating, that is, how to integrate and evolve a highly differentiated organization, and how to enhance elements of the culture that are congruent with new environmental realities while changing dysfunctional elements of the culture.[20]

A heuristic approach to the Heroic Journey provides a tool that enables experience to inform a conceptual framework in an overt legitimate form, one that is capable of changing dysfunctional aspects of a corporate culture. This view of organizational development is a relatively new field and requires both a conceptual frame and a practical methodology that can handle complexity. Archetypal theory is a construct that can contain the tension of polarities that arise from examining a corporate entity. It can also provide metaphorical language that can reach beyond our ability to articulate; in short, an archetypal approach provides access to the visionary realm of possibility. Using a heuristic method enables both facilitator and the participants to incorporate learning into the methodology itself, providing a flexible container by which to encapsulate and articulate a corporate mythology without diluting its effectiveness. Hillman reminds us that "myths amplify and complicate. They are the path of richness."[21]

This path of richness can lead an individual to an emotional connection with the story, offering the potential of an additional connection to take place between individual and organization to enable an emotional bond in and around the story process itself. Simmons believes that the act of storytelling impact emotional states and offers "emotions redirect thought. People react to facts differently depending on their mood, and your story can *change* their mood."[22] A shift in mood can enable emotional connection, and deepen the relationship between teller and listener.

The economic world has changed substantially into a global marketplace. In order to survive such a paradigm shift, we need a new way of looking at organizational development. That perspective must come from the imaginal realm of archetypal psychology. Only a mythic imagination can hold the multiplicity of global perspectives. The Heroic Journey as an operational model provides a rich image that can be amplified across cultural barriers.

So How Does It Work?

To hold a space where creativity can flourish is challenging. Our society is conditioned to act, sometimes in haste. Usually in a reactive stance, an either/or option is frequently available. The challenge lies in the shift to a both/and stance, where duality does not prevent potential to surface out of the depths. Ensuring that employees have a voice provides for greater capacity in innovation. It also removes the emphasis that only leaders can innovate. Gord Huston concurs and states:

> The real breakthrough for Envision was gaining a deeper understanding of the environment within which we operate and how important thought leadership and innovation will be for our future. It is true that the CEO can have a firm grasp of the industry trends and strategic issues, but is not likely the smartest person in the room when it comes to innovation. This point is really made to underline the importance of creating an environment where people feel free to think about new ways of doing what we do.

Taking the time to consider previous actions or processes can be invaluable. Reflection can lead to a psychological breakthrough by which an initial insurmountable problem can be overcome. The importance of telling and re-telling corporate stories allows for employee ownership and the space for breakthroughs to occur. The following example can be found in most organizations. Corporations have gone to great expense to construct a "brand." A sustainable brand comes from within the organization from the heads and more importantly, the hearts of the employees. If you are not living your brand, you don't have one. Another merged example from various organizations will serve to illustrate this point.

An organization had undergone a process whereby stories were collected from all employees to illustrate the essence, or soul, of the organization. The process had been managed by a large advertising agency that wanted to utilize the power of story as a marketing tool. The process took place over several years. Thousands of stories were collected from all employees and then narrowed down to a few hundred for illustrative purposes. Those stories were then "interpreted" by the advertising agency and compiled into a single version, which was then used to form the basis for an advertising campaign.

The employees were demoralized and skeptical of the organization's approach to the use of this all-encompassing "story" for it had no organizational life. Instead, it belonged to the advertising agency. Senior management wanted to know what had gone wrong in this process.

The organizational team was pulled together for a session to discuss the process. Image was again used to facilitate imaginal thinking. Initially, resistance was strong to the approach. The team felt that they had been through this type of work before and that the advertising agency in question had misrepresented the data collected. In heated discussions, various members of the staff decided that the best description of the process undertaken was a theft or betrayal. At this point, I felt that an archetype of transformation had been uncovered—the archetypal of betrayal—and asked for images to be selected that represented this betrayal. The staff was also asked to select an image that might be used to heal this betrayal through the original wound, the theft of the story.

The images of betrayal were then organized into a group and placed on a whiteboard. The team was then broken into smaller groups to explore collectively the images retained that represented an aspect of healing the previous process. Individual worked with their own image and presented to the small group ideas that flowed from the image selected. Each small group then collectively decided upon an approach that could be used to bring the story back to the main body of employees. These various approaches were then presented to the entire team, table by table. All members were asked to reflect upon the ideas generated as a result of the group's consideration of the previous process.

After a couple of weeks, further discussion took place regarding the first session. The team had decided to fire the previous advertising agency and hire a new one. The consensus was that the previous agency had attempted to 'steal' the story, which resulted in the production of an artifact, a story without life. To utilize the concept of story properly, the team decided that the story must stay within the control of the employees as the story itself was fluid, ongoing and still forming. The team recognized the error in judgment made and an apology was extended to the employees. A commitment was also made by the team that the story and its telling would come in the future from the employees. A new advertising campaign would be initiated that truly represented the soul of the organization. The care and feeding of the soul of the organization was returned to its creators, the employees.

The organizational story itself has been brought back to life. Where it will lead, is a future story in the making.

Notes: Breakthrough—Reflection:

1. Jung, CW8: 241.

2. Ibid.

3. Jung, The Undiscovered Self, 41.

4. Hillman, Kinds of Power, 21.

5. Ibid, 232.

6. Bachelard, On Poetic Imagination and Reverie, 14.

7. Hillman, Re-Visioning Psychology, 9.

8. Jung, CW8: 243.

9. Bachelard, 27.

10. Ibid, 21.

11. Hillman, Healing Fiction, 94.

12. Simmons, 45.

13. Von Franz, Archetypal Patterns in Fairy Tales, 16.

14. Ibid, 21.

15. Simmons, 51.

16. Von Franz, 76.

17. Simmons, 54.

18. Ibid.

19. Hillman, Kinds of Power, 51.

20. Schein, Corporate Culture Survival Guide, 144.

21. Hillman, Kinds of Power, 102.

22. Simmons, 78.

Celebration—Creativity

To stay within the experience of the Heroic Journey allows individuals the time to reflect on their own life, the journey experienced so far and where the individual might like the journey to change. Recognizing that a "deepening" is required, to go within and explore beyond the realm of the ego as well as outwardly in seeking a variety of experience, offers a welcome invitation to most individuals.

Fellow travelers are needed who will help build a different society, where people can live and work, play and recreate, learn and grow in an environment that supports individuation. Both my research and my experience to date reinforce the notion that such a process of individuation will produce organizations that are sustainable over time. The process of individuation supports sustainable relationship whether in professional or personal life. Sustainability, as a function of relationship, has the potential not only to build better organizations but also to build a better world.

To work from a mythic perspective, to incorporate both image and thought as opposing forces that may be brought to an act of creation through the transcendent function is equally work and play that is self-fulfilling. To stay in the myth allows the participants a more relaxed psychological state, a return to a child-like innocence that encourages possibility rather than limitation. Story encourages a less analytical, more receptive consciousness that permits a message to enter conscious awareness. James Hillman reminds us that image-making is a royal road to soul-making.[1] Although "soul-making" may be a term that is problematic in an organizational context, it has been my experience that once individuals have had the opportunity to participate in the dialogue between image and thought, such language comes much more easily.

The path of individuation is the path of a leader. To choose the path of individuation is to choose a path that is particular to oneself. Allies may be present or not, the path initially may be a lonely one for each individual must leave the comfort of the collective that is safe, known, and familiar. Thus, the initial question that starts the individual on the journey, the call that beckons, that supplies an answer or at least a direction for: "What do you hunger for that you cannot name?"

Creative ideas come in many forms. To use an archetypal approach permits a holding of the tension between image and thought, matter and energy while encouraging the Self to emerge from the depths forged by experience. Hillman suggests:

> Ideas allow us to envision, and by means of vision we can know. Psychological ideas are ways of seeing and knowing soul, so that a change in psychological ideas means a change in regard to soul and regard for soul.[2]

To know the soul, as Hillman suggests, is necessary for individuation to begin. Whether the process of individuation is ever completed is not important, the emphasis is on process not product, on journey not on destination. Knowing who you are and being true to the Self, transcending the daily debates with the ego, having a level of personal comfort that no person, circumstance, nor opportunity, crisis, nor challenge will dislodge is the core sense of intimately knowing the soul.

Individuation is an invaluable tool in the act of leadership. Knowing that core sense of soul and allowing that sense to provide intuitive direction and guidance, is indispensable to a leader. Knowing that sense of soul, as a leader directs and stewards the process of change, is the most important aspect of leadership.

The task of individuation makes the process of leadership personal. It is not disconnected from the person, the people or the organization. It allows a leader to focus his or her personal talents on a goal. Hillman states "creative people are occupied not so much with creativity as they are fascinated with an opus."[3] To participate in the Heroic Journey is to participate in an opus, to make a life into a creative work of art. Hillman continues to claim that creativity as an instinct is "a necessity of life, and the satisfaction of its needs a requirement for life. In the human being, creativity, like the other instincts, requires fulfillment."[4] He clearly supports Jung's hypothesis: "Consequently, we are led to state that Jungian psychology is based primarily upon the creative instinct and in turn to infer that Jungian psychology is primarily a creative psychology."[5] As such, a creative psychology has much to offer the world of business by acting as a catalyst for innovation.

As most individuals spend at least half of their life at work, then their work, however an individual may define it, is a major element in the opus. For an organization, the issue does not lie in identifying creative individuals but in promoting creativity from all employees. It is much easier to see the *costs* of employees than the *benefits* they offer, which may be indirect or delayed. Is there a way to promote creativity from all employees? Is creativity really of value?

The Rise of the Creative Class

Richard Florida, the H. John Heinz II Professor of Regional Economic Development at the Heinz School of Public Policy and Management at Carnegie-Mellon University would answer a definitive "yes" to both questions. In his book, *The Rise of the Creative Class*, he outlines what he terms a new social class, the Creative Class.

> If you are a scientist or engineer, an architect or designer, a writer, artist or musician, or if you use your creativity as a key factor in your work in business, education, health care, law or some other profession, you are a member. With 38 million members, more than 30 percent of the nation's workforce, the Creative Class has shaped and will continue to shape deep and profound shifts in the ways we work, in our values and desires, and in the very fabric of our everyday lives.[6]

Florida states that the creative impulse, "the attribute that distinguishes us, as humans, from other species—is now being let loose on an unprecedented scale."[7] Few organizations would need a formal study to convince them that creativity, the source of innovation, is important to long-term survival. When people discuss creativity in organizations, it is usually in the context of some *other* company. Rarely do individuals bring up examples from their *own* companies. Perhaps an appropriate analogy would be fish swimming in a body of water. Rarely does the fish recognize the presence of water, as it is part of what is considered normal or routine. Most creative acts do not result from detailed planning but from an atmosphere that encourages and promotes creative thinking. Florida emphasizes that "creativity comes from people. And while people can be hired and fired, their creative capacity cannot be bought or sold, or turned on and off at will."[8] He breaks down his class components by current occupations as shown as follows:[9]

Creative Class and Occupations

Creative Class	Occupations
Super-Creative Core	• Computer and mathematical
	• Architecture and engineering
	• Life, physical, and social science
	• Education, training and library
	• Arts, design, entertainment, sports and media occupations
Creative Professionals	• Management
	• Business and financial operations
	• Legal
	• Healthcare practitioners and technical
	• High-end sales and sales management
Working Class	• Construction and extraction
	• Installation, maintenance and repair
	• Production
	• Transportation and material moving

Creative Class	Occupations
Service Class	• Health care support
	• Food preparation and food-service related
	• Building and grounds cleaning and maintenance
	• Personal care and service
	• Low-end sales
	• Office and Administrative support
	• Community and Social Services
	• Protective service
Agriculture	• Farming, fishing and forestry

If individuation includes, but is not limited to, the ability of an individual to rise above the collective mass, then to enhance the working environment in such a way as to promote and encourage creativity will not only aid in the process of individuation but will also provide a path for corporate success and well-being. If Jung's hypothesis is correct, then creativity is present in every human being, not just a select few. Such realization may have a welcome impact on organizations, as only a fraction of the creative potential contained within the intellectual capital of that organization is being realized. Some organizations will desire to remain in this state of unrealized potential. Time will tell whether those organizations will survive. For organizations that recognize the paradigm shift that is occurring and choose to acknowledge the demographic realities, investing in intellectual capital will become a priority. In other words, the importance of locating and recognizing hidden talent or potential in a responsive organization will be of concern to top management.

Florida states that over 30% of the population in the United States could be considered part of the creative class. Such ranks are rapidly growing as indicated hereafter.

Percentage of Population in Creative Class[10]

Share	Employees (OES data)	Percent Share	Employees (Emp. & Earnings data)	Percent Share
Creative Class	38,278,110	30.0%	38,453,000	28.8%
Super-Creative Core	14,932,420	11.7%	14,133,000	10.6%
Other Creative	23,345,690	18.3%	24,320,000	18.2%
Working Class	33,238,810	26.1%	32,760,000	24.5%
Service Class	55,293,720	43.4%	58,837,000	44.1%
Agriculture	463,360	00.4%	3,426,000	2.6%
Total	127,274,00		133,488,000	

Note: The 1999 *Employment and Earnings* data add to slightly less than total because some occupations are not listed. The OES data omits agricultural workers, so only those in agriculturally related employment are included.

Sources: U.S. Bureau of the Census, *Statistical Abstract of the United States, 2000,* Washington, D.C., 2000, Table 669; U.S. Bureau of Labor Statistics, Occupation and Employment Statistics, 1999, available on-line.

Organizations need to strive to create workplaces that are more amendable to creative or innovation work. In Florida's words, "access to talented and creative people is to modern business what access to coal and iron was to steelmaking."[11] To encourage creativity in any organization is not just of value to the knowledge workers within, it is simply good business strategy. Florida believes we are on the verge of a new lifestyle or paradigm shift which supports the increasing reality of globalization in organizations. Cultural diversity is a welcome addition to the ranks of knowledge workers as such diversity brings differences in approach and opinion. Florida elaborates:

> Whereas the lifestyle of the previous organizational age emphasized conformity, the new lifestyle favours individuality, self-statement, acceptance of difference and the desire for rich multidimensional experiences.[12]

To enable an organization to handle this diversity, communication skills become paramount. If this diversity of approach is handled with care and respect,

Florida believes a multiplicity of views can be collected and examined for organizational use:

> Powering the great ongoing changes of our time is the rise of human creativity as the defining feature of economic life. Creativity has come to be valued—and systems have evolved to encourage and harness it—because new technologies, new industries, new wealth and all other good economic things flow from it. And as a result, our lives and society have begun to resonate with a creative ethos. [13]

The research conducted by Florida isolated workplace attributes that were distinctive in the creative class. These attributes mimic the process of individuation.

Workplace Attributes that Mimic the Individuation Process[14]

Job Factors and Workplace Attributes	
Challenge and responsibility	Being able to contribute and have impact; knowing that one's work makes a difference
Flexibility	A flexible schedule and a flexible work environment; the ability to shape one's work to some degree.
A Stable Work Environment and a Relatively Secure Job	Not lifetime.
Compensation	Especially base pay and core benefits; money you can count on.
Professional Development	The chance to learn and grow, to expand one's horizon for the future.
Peer Recognition	The chance to win the esteem and recognition of others in the know.
Stimulating Colleagues and Managers	Creative people like to be around other creative people, and they prefer leaders who neither micromanage nor ignore them.
Exciting Job Content	The chance to work on projects and technologies that break new ground or pose interesting intellectual problems.

Organizational Culture	An elusive term that can include some factors already mentioned, plus more; perhaps best put for now as simply a culture in which the person feels at home, valued and supported.

Celebration and Recognition

Creativity is as much an art form as an instinct. To reawaken the creative ability in each individual was the goal of Michael Ray at the Stanford Graduate School of Business. In 1980, Professor Ray and artist Rochelle Meyers developed the original "Creativity in Business" course for the MBA program at Stanford as they felt that MBA programs were overly quantitative. In addition to achieving the status of one of the most popular courses in the business school over the last twenty-five years, it has also led to three books, an audiocassette program, and a PBS television series. It has received media attention in this country and over the world for its inward approach to consistently bring out people's highest potential and effectiveness in both business and everyday life. In the December 1996 cover story of *Inc. Magazine*, Michael Ray's book was selected as one of the best nine business and management books ever written.[15]

Although Michael Ray has used the Heroic Journey as a basis for the Creativity in Business program, the model itself was underutilized. Further, in my consulting practice, using an archetypal approach deepens the experience for the participant to create a more sustainable learning process.

Jim Collins, first experienced the Creativity in Business program as an MBA student and then as a professor, teaching the Creativity in Business program with Michael Ray while doing his research on *Built to Last*. Collins' book, *Good to Great* outlines some of the initial Creativity in Business process in implementation. Both Ray and Collins focus on a process similar to individuation, albeit by different names. Ray calls it Generative Leadership; Collins calls it Level 5 Leadership. Regardless of the label, the process is to recognize the innate creative aspects in each individual before that same individual can recognize and appreciate those aspects in others. Both Ray and Collins speak to the maximization of potential in the individual. As such, both of these men collaborate the initial research findings of Jung. Jung believes that each individual is driven towards the Self, not as an intellectual formulation but as an experience. Leadership comes from the experience of leadership, the tests and trials that have built character. Jung affirms such an insight:

Human thought cannot conceive any system or final truth that could give the patient what he needs in order to live: that is, faith, hope, love and insight. These four highest achievements of human effort are so many gifts of grace, which are neither to be taught nor learned, neither given nor taken, neither withheld nor earned, since they come through experience, which is something *given*, and therefore beyond the reach of human caprice. Experiences cannot be *made*. [16]

Celebration and Relationship

Hillman reminds us: "since destruction endangers the opus in any creative venture, the question of management becomes paramount." [17] The source of much of the destructive element in an organizational setting can be found in the area of alignment. Because it has to do with the corporate culture, alignment is hard to both define and describe. When it can be found, a strong alignment is all-pervasive, and will affect all aspects of decision-making. An organization can exist without a strong alignment and therefore recommending an alignment process to enhance relationships within the organization can be problematic. As an alignment of the values in action in an organization carry an emotional charge, a command-control approach to alignment will not be effective. Thus, the emphasis on relationships between members of the organization and how they are constructed is crucial for success. To promote an environment that nurtures creativity requires an approach that recognizes the emotional engagement of the participants, an experience that takes place in the heart and mind.

To ask a traditional organization to recognize the hearts and minds of employees is a challenge, but as the research conducted by Collins in *Built to Last* and *Good to Great* indicates, and as Florida believes, creativity can be the force that drives a new economy.

Celebration and Meaning

If individuals are to render their lives meaningful, such meaning will be accomplished by their choices. Jung believes that meaning only comes

> when people feel that they are living the symbolic life, that they are actors in the divine drama. That gives the only meaning to human life; everything else is banal and you can dismiss it. A career, producing of children, all are *maya* [illusion] compared with that one thing, that your life is meaningful. [18]

As part of the task of individuation, people are asked to take responsibility for their own lives and, as part of that responsibility, create meaning. To participate in one's own opus as a driving force towards meaning enables an individual to withstand the crises and frustrations that are a part of every life. To increase conscious awareness that creativity, and thus the potential to initiate new discoveries is resident in every human being, is to understand that psychic wholeness is available to all. To capitalize on the power of storytelling within a family or an organization is to understand the power of unconscious content that, if made conscious, potentially builds and more perhaps more importantly, deepens relationships between the teller and the listener. Jung offers this insight:

> Myths and fairytales give expression to unconscious processes, and their retelling causes these processes to come alive and be recollected, thereby reestablishing the connection between conscious and unconscious. What the separation of the two psychic halves means, the psychiatrist knows only too well. He knows it as dissociation of the personality, the root of all neuroses. [19]

Jung further believes that "all conscious psychic processes may well be causally explicable; but the creative act, being rooted in the immensity of the unconscious, will forever elude our attempts at understanding."[20] To participate in storytelling, to utilize the visual map of the Heroic Journey, creates an environment or pattern of possibility. The respectful power of story can penetrate layers of indifference or neglect. As Jung states:

> People are weary of scientific specialization and rationalism and intellectualism. They want to hear truths that broaden rather than restrict, that do not obscure but enlighten, that do not run off them like water but penetrate them to the marrow. [21]

For the story, like people, can change.

So How Does It Work?

Acts of creativity that lead to innovation in an organization need to be celebrated. If change was an easy process, our organizations would have shifted to this new economy years ago. It is also important to realize that if any organization wants engagement from its employees, the organization needs to celebrate those who serve the organization, and do so in a public forum. It would not hurt most corporate cultures to celebrate more and criticize less.

Again, Gord Huston concurs and states:

> I believe that the most meaningful way that we celebrated EnvisionU and our educational initiatives was to give it high profile, and virtually every communication piece that we created about the organization, be it annual reports, press releases and speeches, EnvisionU was held out as one of the key initiatives of our organization. Internally, during one of our annual Celebration of Excellence evenings, where we turn the spotlight on our people, each and every staff member who attended the event was given an EnvisionU articulation certificate, which recognized their in-house courses taken and identified how these might be put towards credits with our partnering educational institutions.

To establish a "Celebration of Excellence" evening for employees, confirms that the organization lives its brand. They walk the talk. That level of consistency is the foundation of integrity. That consistency also provides safety and respect in the environment—something that is absolutely necessary for creativity to flourish.

To speak in terms of creativity, context is always an important factor. In this next example, the Canadian pilot for the "Creativity in Business" program was being conducted. As part of the process, an assignment was given to the participants to tell a story which would take from five to fifteen minutes in length. This story could be from an organizational context or from a personal context, the decision being left up to the participant. The participants were informed of this task two months in advance, so ample time was provided for reflection and compilation of the story itself.

The process undergone before this last session was constructed to increase personal awareness and understanding of the Self, to ascertain and develop individual strengths and to establish and strengthen leadership abilities of the participants. The entire process from start to finish took place over a five-month period. Psychological testing of the participants included the use of the 20-subscale Myers-Briggs Type Indicator, the Gallup Strengthsfinder, the Fundamental Interpersonal Relations Orientation-Behaviour (FIRO-B), and the Stanford Business School Work/Life Balance Questionnaire. Individual interviews were conducted with each participant before the commencement of the program, to ascertain individual goals and challenges. All of the personal information and psychological data collected was incorporated into the design process in order to maximize the possibility of obtaining the desired creative outcome. The participants were given a series of "live-withs"[22] as a weekly creativity exercise spanning a period of ten weeks. These "live-withs" were designed to promote a change in perspective, in other words, to change the lens normally used to view day-to-day life.

Resistance by the participants developed fairly quickly around the task of storytelling. The simple act of telling a story produced considerable anxiety, because the stories being developed became highly personal to the participants. It was interesting to note that not one participant chose to tell a story that did not have considerable personal significance. Because the stories involved personal disclosure in an organizational setting, anxiety levels remained high. Participants were repeatedly told that they were responsible for not moving outside their individual comfort level and that coaching would be provided to assist them in developing the story to be told using the Heroic Journey as a frame for their experience.

Specific instructions were provided as follows:

You have each been asked to tell a story—a story about the central questions of the program: "Who is my Self?" and "What is my Work?" It is a story of who you are as a leader and a person, claiming your personal power on your unique Hero/ine's Journey.

Some of your journey "maps" include the Call and the Ordeal of the Hero/ine's Journey, the creativity tools and challenges—all the live-withs you've lived with so far—your values and those of the organizations you are involved with, self-assessment of your personal leadership qualities (the Strengths, the Myers-Briggs Type Indicator, the FIRO-B) and conversations you have had with your peers and your coach.

Here is a reminder of what you might want to think about. You will tell a 5-15 minute story. It can be about anything you want that conveys you as a leader and as a person. You may find yourself focusing on or remembering a significant encounter or event, recent or past (even from childhood) that "sums it up." If so, tell us about it.

- *Think of your storytelling as a creative presentation. Have fun with it. Pull out the stops and experiment.*

- *What have you learned about yourself through the CiB process? What has remained the same, but perhaps you see it with new eyes?*

- *Anchor your story for the listeners. Often, creating the details of a tangible place and time where something significant happened for you makes the story richer for your listeners. What incident, interaction, conversation has occurred for you that represents or 'validates' your image of your Self and your Work? It may be a recent event or realization; or it may be something from the past that takes on a new and deeper meaning for you. Tell an event as it happened to you, or fictionalize it if you like. If there are 'characters' in your story, try portraying them (their moods, voice, how they stand or move).*

- *If you would like to use props, costume elements or anything that would tickle your fancy in the telling, feel free!*[23]

Storytelling coaching was provided by the consultants, (Cheryl de Ciantis and myself), prior to the storytelling exercise. Specific tools were provided to the participants that were practiced in dyads before the commencement of the storytelling process. Suggestions for change were not called for; instead, appreciations of the efforts of the teller were encouraged.

Time arrived for the participants to tell the stories that had been chosen. In this type of work, it is imperative for the facilitators to create an environment of psychological safety. Every effort was made to make the participants as comfortable as possible so the storytelling session might begin.

Over the past several months, individual coaching had been provided to each participant. Practice sessions had been arranged and feedback models provided that allowed this group to practice and learn storytelling skills without impacting the organization. Instead, the group participated in the training exercises which allowed the individual participants to develop new norms and assumptions around the process of creative leadership and personal development together as a group. As such, each participant provided a positive role model for the other participants so that each person could see what a new way of thinking looks and feels like before attempting to teach others the same process. The group became its own support reference and was able to talk freely about the frustrations and difficulties involved in learning how to expand conscious awareness in an organizational setting.

The specific details of the stories told are confidential and will remain so, but it can be said that the process was more successful than the facilitators had anticipated. Each teller became completely engaged with the story being presented. The telling was not just an intellectual exercise, but an emotional experience for all. Most stories lasted the fully allotted time or exceeded the original maximum specified. No effort was made to cut the story short. Instead, each participant was allowed to experience fully the process intellectually and emotionally.

As a result, the participants formed a much closer relationship with each other and had a fuller, more expansive understanding of both the professional and personal competence held by each individual in the group.

The important teaching for any consultant who wishes to attempt this process is to stay out of the way. Recognition, relationship, and meaning with respect to the Self and to Others will become evident in the story.

Notes: Celebration—Creativity

1. Hillman, Re-Visioning Psychology, 23.

2. Ibid, 121.

3. Hillman, Myth of Analysis, 20.

4. Ibid, 33.

5. Hillman, Myth of Analysis, 34.

6. Florida, The Rise of the Creative Class, ix. This is a fascinating look at the emerging field of knowledge workers that are rapidly increasing within our organizations. When this class of workers leave the office every night, the assets of the organization leave with them. Your assets now have feet!

7. Ibid, 4.

8. Ibid, 5.

9. Ibid, 328.

10. Ibid, 330.

11. Ibid, 6.

12. Ibid, 13.

13. Ibid, 21.

14. Ibid, 92.

15. See "Creativity in Business" by Michael Ray. This book was written in 1984 and is still used as a foundational resource. See also Ray's latest book, "The Highest Goal", 2005, an excellent reference for developing core values in the workplace. Ray was a pioneer in bringing spirituality into organizations.

16. Jung, Modern Man in Search of a Soul, 226.

17. Hillman, Myth of Analysis, 38.

18. Jung, CW18: 630.

19. Jung, CW9i: 280.

20. Jung, CW15: 135.

21. Jung, CW15: 86.

22. See "The Highest Goal" by Michael Ray for a description and list of live-withs that have been used in an organizational setting. These live-withs are designed to provide an experience of your own rigid thinking and ways to get outside your own pattern. One such live-with that caused me great personal torment was "Have No Expectations." I lost sleep over attempting to incorporate it into my daily behaviour. When I turn on a lightswitch, I expect…When I turn on my computer to write, I expect…When I shut my eyes, I expect to wake up. You see my problem! I heartily recommend using this technique, even though it has turned my hair gray in some situations.

23. This process was constructed and designed by organizational consultant Cheryl De Ciantis, my partner in the Canadian pilot. She is a joy to work with and brilliant in her intuitive understanding of the creative process.

Re-Visioning

In the fall of 2002, I began a post-doctoral teacher/training course with Michael Ray at the Stanford Graduate School of Business. This training was to prepare the participants to teach the "Creativity in Business" program. I had already decided to pursue the world of business in writing my dissertation but my experiences in this course solidified my intent. The setting of the Faculty Club at Stanford University was intimidating but equally incredibly rewarding. Being part of the teacher/trainer group changed my life: It enabled me to be comfortable in my own skin.

The Heroic Journey is used as a visual representation in the course. But my experience was that the program did not do the model justice—the model needed deepening to mine its true richness. The impact that mythologist Joseph Campbell had on many people through his books and various television documentaries such as *The Power of Myth* with Bill Moyers, continues to grow. The work of Michael Ray and those that have assisted him over the past quarter-century have certainly invited mythology to enter the complex world of business. Although the program itself is an experiential one, deepening of the process was needed to produce a greater impact.

My experience as a graduate student at Pacifica Graduate Institute confirmed my intuitive sense that mythology can bring great riches to the world of organizations and corporate life. I am also convinced that archetypal psychology has the power and the sensitivity to bring about change in a corporate environment. This book is my attempt to merge the two: Campbell's visual map and Jung and the post-Jungians' influence on the reality of the psyche.

This work is a hypothesis, a statement of theory that has yet to be fully explored and, more importantly, continually tested in practical terms. My experience as a consultant leads me to believe that this approach is not only viable, but perhaps the most powerful tool available to effect organizational change. To personify the Heroic Journey is a way of experiencing change that provides a comforting structure in the midst of psychic upheaval. Hillman believes as well that "Personifying is a way of being in the world and *experiencing the world as a psychological field*, where persons are given with events, so that events are experiences that touch us, move us, appeal to us."[1] Using the Heroic Journey to contain my understanding of Jung and the process of individuation, touches others at a deep level and makes the process of change more appealing. It is my aim to continue this work, to further the research that will support my findings and perhaps inspire others to venture into the corporate fray. A discussion around traditional management theory, and with it, the way people are treated on a day-to-day basis in our organizations, is now underway. To recognize the archetypal power of recognition, relationship, and meaning as the primary concerns of our race, is, to support the process of individuation and not to manage it. On the use of power, Hillman offers a cogent comment:

> The power to conceive, to carry to term and give birth to, and then nourish, protect and enhance another life shows an everyday kind of incomparable agency, literally as mother and metaphorically as a way of exercising power elsewhere. To sustain continuity, to uphold ideals and values, to feed whatever one is responsible for so that it flourishes, sometimes at the cost of your own lessening, is not to idealize motherhood but to recognize an archetypal model of power that rarely finds its way into the teaching texts of management with their focus on assertiveness skills, confrontation with insubordination and image projection.[2]

To re-vision the role of the Hero/ine in corporate life is to re-vision our view of human potential in an organization. To make the move away from power-driven, command-control thinking to a more participatory view enables individuals to publicly utilize personal creativity that supports corporate innovation. There will always be some people for which individuation is not desirable. There will always be some corporations that exist for the sole purpose of profit at whatever cost. But if profitability can also be realized while maximizing intellectual capital in an organization, perhaps this ability to nurture the instinct of creativity will prevail.

That is my hope and my wish. Jung has taught us that change must begin with the individual. With the increasing popularity of the myth of the Hero/ine, perhaps this rise of the Hero/ine announces a collective shift towards the process of individuation. In the words of Marie-Louise von Franz, "one of the characteristics of a civilization on the rise is that, in general, all of the different fields of life—law, religion, political order, social order, art, etc.—express the same symbol. They are all on the same wavelength."[3]

Perhaps it is projection on my part that individuals respond to the Heroic Journey because the collective as a whole is tending towards that symbol. As a means of facing the challenges ahead of a reduced workforce through our current demographic shift and economic globalization, the integration of one's own individual myth with that of an organization provides a relational framework by which both individual and organization can realize creative potential in a win/ win environment.

Conscious use of an archetype of transformation such as the Heroic Journey resonates with individuals. As an archetype of transformation, the Heroic Journey is capable of bridging the gap between two individuals or two corporate cultures, as in the case of a merger or acquisition (M&A's). It is wise to learn as much as possible about a potential mate before marriage, and the same can be said about a possible partner in a merger. A complete transformation of two companies into a new organization requires a deep understanding of capabilities and resources. A cultural due diligence, or examination of corporate culture, is often overlooked, in part because of the lack of required assessment capabilities. Archetypal psychology has much to offer this process. There is a crucial link between employee commitment and emotional engagement and successful implementation of corporate strategy. As corporate assets now consist primarily of intellectual capital, retention of that capital is a necessary goal of management and critical to the long-term success of the organization.

By use of archetypal theory, a statistical form of cultural measurement, and the use of the power of story, a cultural alignment can be performed to enable the retention of intellectual capital as part of the merger process. Cultural issues may be an important factor in domestic mergers, but such issues are compounded when the cultures of different countries are considered. The role of a archetypal consultant is invaluable in the process because she or he brings specific expertise to bridging these cultural variances. Integration is an on-going process, but as seen in the examples offering throughout the foregoing chapters, integration is not only possible but probable if archetypal factors are brought into the process. Alignment and integration lead to full engagement across the organization.

To bring the importance of mergers and acquisitions into perspective, some statistical data may be of assistance:

The 1980s produced approximately 55,000 mergers and acquisitions in the United States alone. The value of the acquisitions during this decade was approximately $1.3 trillion. As impressive as these numbers are, they are small in comparison to the merger wave that began in the earlier 1990s, approximately in 1993. The number and value of mergers and acquisitions have grown each year since 1993. For example, in 1997, there were approximately 22,000 mergers and acquisitions, roughly 40 percent of the total during the whole decade of the 1980s. Perhaps more important, the value of mergers and acquisitions in 1997 was $1.6 trillion. [...] Approximately $2.5 trillion in mergers and acquisitions were announced in 1999, continuing the upward trend. [4]

It is easy to forget among the statistics and dollar volume that mergers and acquisitions refer to people, thousands of them, who are affected by this type of business activity. The dollar volume cited becomes even more disturbing when the facts indicate that "mergers and acquisitions have understandably gotten a bad name. Bad numbers underscore M&A's sour reputation. History has shown that 35% to 50% of all deals ultimately fail."[5] The failure rates do not begin to represent the impact upon the individuals within those organizations.

To find an approach that will directly influence the above results will serve world economy, our business communities, and the individuals within them. As such, the use of the Heroic Journey as a tool for transformation may have lasting significance. It is not my intention to review the history of mergers and acquisitions. Suffice to say that an opportunity exists for archetypal theory to be utilized in strategically enhancing the success rate of such business enterprise. Notwithstanding the impact on the organizations concerned, the impact on the people that make up the organization is far more important because they represent the long-term viability of any organization. Sustainability through investment in human capital will be a touchstone for the successful organizations of the future.

Perhaps Gord Huston says it best:

> Our new insights at Envision continue to evolve. Our spirit of innovation continues to grow and does receive nurturing from our Board and Executive Team. In fact our current initiative is to send three thought leaders on what we are calling a Columbus Expedition to visit thought leaders in the area of innovation. One truism of many organizations is that they have a strong desire, but do not necessarily know how to be innovative. Our Columbus project will allow us to learn from the best and, if we get it right, incorporate this into the Envision Culture.
>
> [...] I would say to you that EnvisionU, while interesting, it is certainly revolutionary and newsworthy and is one good thing, but the real Envision story is around recognizing that success in business is no longer possible with a command-and-control philosophy. For most organizations this thinking is no longer in step with the market dynamics of today's changing economy. People at all parts of the organization must understand the Vision, embrace the values and feel engaged in and supportive of the objectives of the organization. This

is a very difficult thing to accomplish, but when it is there, companies move from good to great.

In order for people at all parts of the organization to truly understand the vision, they must have a hand in its creation. The vision may be driven by the executive but with an employee voice in implementation from the bottom up. Continued work in this area is intended by myself and associates.

Our approach is fourfold. A shift towards a more humane culture in organizations that supports both internal and external branding will be comprised of the following aspects:

1. use of image to access archetypal forces within individuals and thus within the corporate culture;

2. a measurement tool such as the Q12 devised by Gallup to provide a baseline for comparative analysis;

3. use of an archetypal model such as the Heroic Journey by which an individual or corporate culture can produce desired change; and

4. both storytelling and continued use of image as a communication tool to facilitate the process and create a sustainable brand.

We need to re-vision the way we work. To open the mind to the power of story as an archetypal force is to allow the power of the mythic imagination to break through. Perhaps the purpose in human life is to help creation and all acts of creativity by being the agent of consciousness and in the act of storytelling, carry the fertile seeds for a viable future both for organizations and the human race.

Notes: Re-Visioning

1. Hillman, Re-Visioning Psychology, 13.

2. Hillman, Kinds of Power, 209.

3. Von Franz, 24.

4. Hitt, Harrison and Ireland, 4.

5. Clemente and Greenspan, 2.

Bibliography

Aristotle. *Poetics*. Trans. Malcolm Heath. London: Penguin, 1996.

Bachelard, Gaston. *On Poetic Imagination and Reverie*. Trans. Colette Gaudin. Rev. ed. Dallas: Spring 1974.

Bakan, Joel. *The Corporation: The Pathological Pursuit of Profit and Power*. Toronto: Penguin Group, 2004.

Barnhart, Robert K. *The Barnhart Concise Dictionary of Etymology. The Origins of American English Words*. New York: HarperCollins, 1995.

Baumard, Philipe. *Tacit Knowledge in Organizations*. Trans. Samantha Wauchope. Thousand Oaks: Sage, 1999.

Bohm, David. *Quantum Theory*. New York: Dover, 1951.

Bohr, Neils. "Truth Dwells in the Deeps." *Quantum Questions*, Ed. Ken Wilber. 1984. Boston: Shambhala, 33-38.

Bond, D. Stephenson. *Living Myth: Personal Meaning as a Way of Life*. Boston: Shambhala, 1993.

Buckingham, Marcus, and Curt Coffman. *First, Break all the Rules*. New York: Simon & Shuster, 1999.

Buckingham, Marcus, and Donald O. Clifton. *Now, Discover Your Strengths*. New York: Simon & Shuster, 2001.

Campbell, Joseph. *Pathways to Bliss: Mythology and Personal Transformation*. Ed. David Kudler. Novato: New World Library, 2004.

—. *The Hero With a Thousand Faces*. 2nd Ed. Princeton: Princeton UP, 1968.

Canada Business Corporations Act, 1997. 16th Ed. Toronto: Thomson Professional Publishing, 1996.

Clemente, Mark N., and David S. Greenspan. *Winning at Mergers and Acquisitions. The Guide to Market-Focused Planning and Integration.* New York: John Wiley & Sons, 1998.

Collins, James C. *Good to Great.* New York: HarperCollins, 2001.

Collins, James C., and Jerry I. Porras. *Built to Last.* New York: HarperCollins, 1994.

Deal, Terrence E., and Allan H. Kennedy. *Corporate Cultures. The Rites and Rituals of Corporate Life.* Cambridge: Perseus, 1982.

—. *The New Corporate Cultures. Revitalizing the Workplace after Downsizing, Mergers, and Reengineering.* Cambridge: Perseus, 1999.

De Ciantis, Cheryl. What Does Drawing My Hand Have to Do with Leadership? A Look at the Process of Leaders Becoming Artists. *The Journal of Aesthetic Education* 30 (1996). 87-97.

Drucker, Peter F. *The Essential Drucker.* New York: HarperBooks, 2001.

Dychtwarld, Ken, Tamara Erickson, and Bob Morison. It's Time to Retire Retirement. *Harvard Business Review,* 2004. Art. Reprint R0403C.

Ellwood, Robert. *The Politics of Myth. A Study of C.G. Jung, Mircea Eliade and Joseph Campbell.* Albany: SUNY, 1999.

Florida, Richard. *The Rise of the Creative Class and How its Transforming Work, Leisure, Community and Everyday Life.* New York: Basic Books, 2002.

Fogel, Robert. *The Fourth Great Awakening and the Future of Egalitarianism.* Chicago: Chicago UP, 2000.

Giegerich, Wolfgang. *The Soul's Logical Life. Towards a Rigorous Notion of Psychology.* Frankfurt: Peter Lang GmbH, 1999.

Haft, Robert J. *Due Diligence in Securities Transactions.* St. Paul: West Group Securities Law Series, 2000-2001.

Hawking, Stephen. *A Brief History of Time.* New York: Bantam, 1988.

Heifetz, Ronald A. *Leadership Without Easy Answers*. Cambridge: Harvard UP, 1994.

Hillman, James. *Healing Fiction*. New York: Stanton Hill, 1983.

—. *Insearch: Psychology and Religion*. 2nd ed. Woodstock. Spring, 1994.

—. *Kinds of Power. A Guide to its Intelligent Uses*. New York: Doubleday. 1995.

—. *Re-Visioning Psychology*. New York: Harper, 1975.

—. *The Myth of Analysis*. New York: HarperCollins, 1972.

Hitt, Michael A., Jeffery S. Harrison, and R. Duane Ireland. *Mergers and Acquisitions: A Guide to Creating Value for Stakeholders*. Oxford: Oxford UP, 2001.

Izzo, John B., and Pam Withers. *Values Shift: The New Work Ethic and What it Means for Business*. Toronto: Prentice Hall, 2000.

Jung, C. G. Aion. Researches into the Phenomenology of the Self. Trans. R. F. C. Hull. *The Collected Works of C. G. Jung*. CW 9ii. Bollingen Series 20. Princeton: Princeton UP, 1959. 2nd ed. 1969.

—. The Archetypes and the Collective Unconscious. Trans. R. F. C. Hull. *The Collected Works of C. G. Jung*. CW 9i. Bollingen Series 20. Princeton: Princeton UP, 1959. 2nd ed. 10th Printing 1990.

—. *C. G. Jung: Letters*. Volume 1. Selected and Edited by Gerhard Adler and Aniela Jaffe. Princeton. Princeton UP, 1973.

—. Freud and Psychoanalysis. Trans. R. F.C. Hull. *The Collected Works of C. G. Jung*. CW 4. Princeton: Princeton UP, 1967.

—. *Memories, Dreams, Reflections*. Trans. Richard and Clara Winston. New York: Random House Inc., 1989.

—. *Modern Man in Search of a Soul*. Trans. W. S. Dell and Cary F. Baynes. New York: Harvest/HBJ Books, 1933.

—. The Practice of Psychotherapy. Trans. R. F. C. Hull. *The Collected Works of C. G. Jung*. CW 16. Bollingen Series 20. Princeton: Princeton UP, 1954. 2nd ed. 1966.

—. Psychology and Alchemy. Trans. R. F. C. Hull. *The Collected Works of C. G. Jung.* CW 12. Bollingen Series 20. Princeton: Princeton UP, 1953, 2nd ed. 1968.

—. Psychology and the West. Trans. R. F. C. Hull. *The Collected Works of C. G. Jung.* CW 11. Bollingen Series 20. Princeton: Princeton UP, 1958, Paperback ed. 1984.

—. Psychological Types. Trans. R. F. C. Hull. *The Collected Works of C. G. Jung.* CW 6. Bollingen Series 20. Princeton: Princeton UP, 1921. 2nd ed. 1974, 9th Printing, 1990.

—. *Psyche and Symbol.* Trans. R. F. C. Hull. Princeton: Princeton UP, 1958.

—. *Seminar on Nietzsche's Zarathustra.* Edited and abridged by James L. Jarrett. Princeton: Princeton UP, 1998.

—. The Spirit in Man, Art, and Literature. Trans. R. F. C. Hull. *The Collected Works of C. G. Jung.* CW 15. Bollingen Series 20. Princeton: Princeton UP, 1966. 4th ed. 1978.

—. The Structure and Dynamics of the Psyche. Trans. R. F. C. Hull. *The Collected Works of C. G. Jung.* CW 8. Bollingen Series 20. Princeton: Princeton UP, 1960. 2nd ed. 1969.

—. The Symbolic Life. Trans. R. F. C. Hull. *The Collected Works of C. G. Jung.* CW 18. Princeton: Princeton UP, 1955. 3rd ed. 1989.

—. Symbols of Transformation. Trans. R. F. C. Hull. *The Collected Works of C. G. Jung.* CW 5. Bollingen Series 20. Princeton: Princeton UP, 1956. 2nd ed. 1967, 10th Printing, 1990.

—. Two Essays on Analytical Psychology. Trans. R. F. C. Hull. *The Collected Works of C. G. Jung.* CW 7. Bollingen Series 20. Princeton: Princeton UP, 1953. 2nd ed. 1966, 4th Printing, 1977.

—. *The Undiscovered Self.* Trans. R. F. C. Hull. Princeton: Princeton UP, 1990.

Moustakas, Clark. *Heuristic Research. Design, Methodology, and Applications.* Newbury Park: Sage, 1990.

Neuhauser, Peg C. *Corporate Legends & Lore: The Power of Storytelling as a Management Tool.* Austin: PCN Associates, 1993.

Nonaka, Ikujiro, and Hirotaka Takeuchi. *The Knowledge-Creating Company.* Oxford: Oxford UP, 1995.

Nonaka, Ikujiro, and Toshihiro Nishiguchi. *Knowledge Emergence: Social, Technological and Evolutionary Dimensions of Knowledge Creation.* Oxford: Oxford UP, 2001.

Ray, Michael. *Creativity in Business.* New York: Broadway Books, 1986.

Schein, Edgar H. *Organizational Culture and Leadership.* 2nd ed. San Francisco: Jossey-Bass, 1992.

—. *The Corporate Culture Survival Guide.* San Francisco: Jossey-Bass Publishers. 1999.

Simmons, Annette. *The Story Factor: Inspiration, Influence, and Persuasion through the Art of Storytelling.* Cambridge: Perseus, 2001.

Wachtman, Edward. "Storytelling: The Narrative Structure of Evaluation." *Communication Strategies in Evaluation.* Ed. Nick L. Smith. Beverly Hills: Sage, 1982. 89-119.

Walker, Steven F. *Jung and the Jungians on Myth.* New York: Garland, 1995.

Von Franz, Marie-Louise. *Archetypal Patterns in Fairy Tales.* Toronto: Inner City, 1997.

Definition of Terms

Central to the work of a depth psychological perspective on organizational development are the concepts of *archetypes, corporations, consciousness, ego, ectopsyche, endopsyche, Heroic Journey, Hero/ine, individuation, knowledge workers, knowledge management, metamythology, self,* and *tacit knowledge.* To bring a mythic approach to organizational development, these terms require some explanation.

The notion of archetype comes from Ancient Greece. *The Barnhart Concise Dictionary of Etymology* translates *arche* as "first" or "primal" and *typos* as "stamp."[1] A theory based on archetypes attempts to access the first ideas, primal imprints, or first principles of humankind. It is from such an in-depth, extensive examination that the phrase "depth or archetypal psychology" originates. C. G. Jung also classified archetypes as having the form as well as the meaning of "mythological motifs," which appeared in pure form in fairytales, myths, legends, and folklore. From an appreciation of the archetypes that move within our own life, we can start to develop a core value system that can govern our behaviour.

A *corporation*, as defined under the Canada Business Corporations Act, is an "individual, partnership, association, body corporate, trustee, executor, administrator or legal representative" (*The Canada Business Corporations Act, 1997.* 16th Edition 3.[3] Corporate law worldwide permits a legal corporation to have the same rights as an individual.

The definition of *conscious* and *ego* will be based in the work of C. G. Jung, who describes them as follows:

> The important fact about consciousness is that nothing can be conscious without an ego to which it refers. If something is not related to the ego then it is not conscious. Therefore you can define consciousness as a relation of psychic facts to the ego. What is that ego? The ego is a complex datum which is constituted first of all by a general awareness of your body, of your existence, and secondly by your memory data; you have a certain idea of having been, a long series of memories. Those two are the main constituents of what we call the ego. Therefore you can call the ego a complex of psychic facts. This complex has a great power of attraction, like a magnet; it attracts contents from the unconscious, from that dark realm of which we know nothing; it also attracts

impressions from the outside, and when they enter into association with the ego they are conscious. If they do not, they are not conscious.[4]

Functions of consciousness, Jung terms *ectopsyche* and *endopsyche*, which allow consciousness to become oriented in the field of ectopsychic and endopsychic facts:

> What I understand by the *ectopsyche* is a system of relationship between the contents of consciousness and the facts and data coming in from the environment. It is a system of orientation which concerns my dealing with the external facts given to me by the function of my senses. The *endopsyche*, on the other hand, is a system of relationship between the contents of consciousness and postulated processes in the unconscious.[5]

Hero's Journey is a term coined by Joseph Campbell in his book, *The Hero with a Thousand Faces*. The term *Heroic Journey* will be used to refer to a path that may be taken by an organization as a description of the phases of development it must pass through in the process of maturation, or in Jungian terms, its individuation. It is useful to note that even though organizations have the legal status and identity of individuals, they are not. Nevertheless, they are populated by individuals who exhibit both personal and organizational development.

Hero/ine is an inclusive term originally coined by Cheryl de Ciantis[6] and will be used to refer to either a male or female Hero.

Individuation, a term coined by Jung, describes the potential life process of an individual if he or she chooses to engage in such activity. Usually, individuation is attempted in the second half of life. Jung defines the process of *individuation* in more detail:

> Since the growth of the personality comes out of the unconscious, which is by definition unlimited, the extent of the personality now gradually realizing itself cannot in practice be limited either. But, unlike the Freudian superego, it is still individual. It is in fact individuality in the highest sense, and therefore theoretically unlimited, since no individual can possibly display *every* quality. (I have called this process of realization the "individuation process."[7]

Knowledge worker is a term originally used by management theorist Peter Drucker. It refers to the mode of production shifting from materials produced by factories to knowledge produced and contained in the mind of the individual worker. In *The Essential Drucker*, he summarizes:

knowledge workers are not subordinates; they are "associates." For, once beyond the apprentice stage, knowledge workers must know more about their job than their boss does—or else they are no good at all. In fact, that they know more about their job than anybody else in the organization is part of the definition of knowledge workers.[8]

Since modes of production have indeed become more information-based, the term will be used extensively throughout this book to refer to employees within any organization.

Knowledge management is the management of information or other data by which knowledge workers accomplish their work.

Metamythology is my coined term representing the psychic drive theory first formulated by Jung. As *drive* is usually paired with Freudian psychology, so that term will be avoided. Instead, *meta* has been added to *mythology* to mean a transcending or more advanced form of mythology, being the incorporation of Jung's theory into the world of story.

The use of the word *Self* will be used as Jung intended, as not being limited to just ego consciousness. In *Transformation Symbolism in the Mass,* Jung elaborates on his definition of the Self:

> [...] the conscious mind is contained like a smaller circle within a larger one. Hence it is quite possible for the ego to be made into an object, that is to say, for a more compendious personality to emerge in the course of development and take the ego into its service. [...] The term "self" seemed to me a suitable one for this unconscious substrate, whose actual exponent in consciousness is the ego. The ego stands to the self as the moved to the mover, or as object to subject, because the determining factors which radiate out from the self surround the ego on all sides and are therefore supraordinate to it. The self, like the unconscious, is an *a priori* existent out of which the ego evolves. It is, so to speak, an unconscious prefiguration of the ego. [9]

Tacit knowledge is knowledge that is undocumented, existing outside the confines of policy and procedure. It includes the wisdom of the body and its experiential voice, the soul. As Philippe Baumard argues in *Tacit Knowledge in Organizations,* "[b]ehind both purposeful and unintentional ambiguities lies a knowledge that cannot be articulated or stabilized. On one hand it is implicit knowledge, that is something we might know, but do not wish to express. On the other hand, it is tacit knowledge, that is something that we know but cannot express."[10] Tacit knowledge might also be expressed in the phrase, "the way things are done around here" and, as such, varies among institutions, organizations and cultures. It has been my experience that tacit knowledge can be found and brought to consciousness through an examination of corporate culture by way of the stories or *mythos* of the organization itself.

1. Barnhart, The Barnhart Concise Dictionary of Etymology, 36. If you ever wanted to own a dictionary for where words originated, this is my pick as the best.

2. Jung, CW18: 80.

    FYI: All references to the main body of the work of C.G. Jung is called the Collected Works (CW). For ease of reference, regardless of which translation from the original German is being used, references are made to paragraph NOT page numbers. So CW18: 80 is Volume 18 of the Collected Works: paragraph number 80. Any other reference to Jung's writings that are not part of the Collected Works will give the title of the book and the page number.

3. Although this describes the Canadian legal definition of a corporation, every country in the world will have a specific definition that is used. All allow a corporation the rights of an individual.

4. Jung, CW18: 18.

5. Jung, CW18: 20.

6. Personal conversations, January 2003.

7. Jung, CW11: 390.

8. Drucker, 78. Peter Drucker is one of the grandfathers of organizational development. His writings span several decades and he is one of the few theorists who continually updates his work, building on previous theories or sometimes, even tearing them down. If you have never read any OD theorist, Drucker is a fine place to start.

9. Jung, CW11: 391.

10. Baumard, 2.

About the Author

After spending more than two decades in management, Ginger followed her dream, quit her job, cashed in her retirement savings and—fuelled by the works of Joseph Campbell and Carl Jung—jumped headlong into the mythic world of story as a student at Pacifica Graduate Institute, the only archetypal graduate school in North America. She did post-doctoral training with Michael Ray, founder of the Stanford MBA program "Creativity in Business" and is the only Canadian in the teacher/ training group created by Michael Ray. She uses her skills and consulting experience to enhance creativity in people and innovation in organizations.

Ginger is an accomplished program designer and facilitator in Jungian-based learning and motivation. Her personal and professional passion is in the stories associated with the archetypal Heroic Journey. An adept teacher and stimulating speaker, Ginger inspires and motivates others to identify and pursue their own unique paths, both professional and personal.

Ginger completed her doctoral dissertation using the Hero's Journey as a tool for personal and professional development, with particular emphasis on issues of corporate culture and employee retention. This is her first book of a series on this theme and interviews are underway for: Re-Visioning Retirement, Leadership: For Women by Women, and Archetypal Branding: From the Inside Out.

Gingers areas of expertise include:

- Identifying, understanding and applying organizational myths and metaphors to affect corporate culture change

- Alignment of vision and values

- Key staff retention and employee engagement

- Storytelling as a developmental and marketing tool

- Applying mythic and archetypal thinking to the art of leadership

- Re-visioning retirement

Although allergic to small boats, Ginger lives in beautiful Vancouver, British Columbia and spends her spare time in reading, cooking sprees, oil-painting landscapes and practicing latin dance.

She can be reached at:
ginger@creativityinbusiness.org
http://www.creativityinbusiness.org

Index

978-0-595-36595-1
0-595-36595-7